Writing to Learn
FROM PARAGRAPH TO ESSAY

Writing to Learn
FROM PARAGRAPH
TO ESSAY

LOU J. SPAVENTA
MARILYNN L. SPAVENTA

Santa Barbara City College

Boston   Burr Ridge, IL   Dubuque, IA   Madison, WI   New York   San Francisco   St. Louis
Bangkok   Bogotá   Caracas   Lisbon   London   Madrid
Mexico City   Milan   New Delhi   Seoul   Singapore   Sydney   Taipei   Toronto

McGraw-Hill Higher Education

A Division of The **McGraw-Hill** *Companies*

WRITING TO LEARN: FROM PARAGRAPH TO ESSAY

 This book is printed on recycled, acid-free paper containing 10% postconsumer waste.

1 2 3 4 5 6 7 8 9 0 QPD/QPD 0 9 8 7 6 5 4 3 2 1 0

ISBN 0–07–230755–2

Vice president and editor-in-chief: *Thalia Dorwick*
Editorial director: *Tina B. Carver*
Director of marketing: *Tom Dare*
Senior project manager: *Peggy J. Selle*
Production supervisor: *Sandy Ludovissy*
Coordinator of freelance design: *David W. Hash*
Cover/text designer: *Juan Vargas*
Cover illustration: *©PhotoDisc Inc., 1999*
Supplement coordinator: *Sandra M. Schnee*
Compositor: *David Corona Design*
Typeface: *11/13 Stone Sans*
Printer: *Quebecor Printing Book Group/Dubuque, IA*

Library of Congress Cataloging-in-Publication Data

Spaventa, Louis J.
   Writing to learn / Louis J. Spaventa, Marilynn L. Spaventa. — 1st ed.
     p.   cm.
   Includes indexes.
   Contents: [bk. 1] The sentence — bk. 2. The paragraph — bk. 3. From paragraph to essay — bk. 4. The essay.
ISBN 0–07–230753–6 (bk.1) — ISBN 0–07–230754–4 (bk. 2) — ISBN 0–07–230755–2 (bk. 3) — ISBN 0–07–230756–0 (bk. 4)
1. English language—Textbooks for foreign speakers.   2. English language—Rhetoric—Problems, exercises, etc.   3. Report writing—Problems, exercises, etc.   I. Spaventa, Marilynn.   II. Title.

PE1128 .S697   2001
808'.042—dc21   99–057820
                                             CIP

www.mhhe.com

CONTENTS

Unit 2: Family and Relationships

Unit 3: Education

Writing to Learn: *From Paragraph to Essay*

Unit 6: The Natural World

Writing to Learn: *From Paragraph to Essay*

To the Instructor

WRITING TO LEARN is a four-book ESL writing series aimed at adult learners of English from diverse educational backgrounds. The series focuses both on the process of writing and on writing as a product. The goal of the series is to help students learn how to write for academic and vocational success. Each book in the series makes use of student skills and experience to generate writing topics while providing guided practice of appropriate vocabulary and grammar, English writing conventions, writing, editing, rewriting, and journal writing. Each chapter of books 1 and 2 and each unit of book 3 in the series begins with a visual image that leads to discussion and writing. The fourth text uses readings as prewriting prompts. WRITING TO LEARN begins with an elementary text designed to improve student ability to write accurate and descriptive English sentences. The upper elementary to intermediate level text focuses on writing paragraphs. The third or intermediate level text takes the student from paragraph writing to organizing, writing, and editing essays. The final book at the advanced level concentrates on improving student essay writing skills and enhancing essay writing style.

Each book in the series is divided into six units. Books 1 and 2, *The Sentence* and *The Paragraph,* have two chapters in each unit while books 3 and 4, *From Paragraph to Essay* and *Writing Essays,* have just six units each. The reason for the difference is to create more and shorter lessons for the elementary to lower intermediate levels, and fewer but longer lessons at the intermediate to advanced levels of writing.

Here are the unit themes:

Unit One: Myself and Others

Unit Two: Family and Relationships

Unit Three: Education

Unit Four: Work

Unit Five: Leisure and Recreation

Unit Six: The Natural World

Students who work through several texts in the series will have the opportunity to explore the same theme from different perspectives.

The use of icons to indicate pair and group work [icons] is meant to facilitate classroom organization while eliminating repetitive instructions—the number indicates the total number of students needed to form the group. You will also notice that exercises use names of students from a variety of cultures, because we recognize that students will use English to communicate with others from diverse ethnic and linguistic groups. Finally, be sure to follow each unit in the Instructor's Edition for helpful suggestions and instructions for activities that are not included in the student text.

Organization

Each unit is divided into the following four sections:

A. Prewriting   In *From Paragraph to Essay,* each unit begins with prewriting activities based on a picture story. Prewriting activities include vocabulary learning, pair work, group work, and discussion. It is important for students to understand writing as a process that begins with creative reflection and communication.

B. Structure   Grammar activities include review of basic English grammar and practice in coordination and subordination. Although the structure section introduces grammar with example, explanation, and practice exercises, *From Paragraph to Essay* is not meant to be a grammar text. Grammar has been incorporated as a tool for expressing one's thoughts rather than as an end in itself.

C. Writing and Editing   Activities in this section are devoted to improving writing skills, especially employing the vocabulary and grammar practiced in sections A and B. Activities in this section develop from controlled to creative practice. You will notice that we have not included sample student paragraphs and essays for students to follow in the writing section. In many texts, writing samples are provided with the expectation that students will diligently work with the sample to produce their own personalized writing. In fact, this rarely happens and students are more likely to be constricted by the model. In this series, the writing models appear in the structure and editing sections to encourage students to alter the samples and make the language their own. Each unit requires an extensive writing and revising assignment. The first three units require coherent, well-organized paragraphs. The fourth unit assigns a three-paragraph letter, and the last two units require five-paragraph essays. All of these assignments should involve at least two drafts and a peer editing phase. You can have students keep these assignments in a folder to develop a portfolio.

D. Journal Assignment   The personal, unedited, daily writing practice that journal writing affords is an important part of the process of writing well in English. There is a variety of journal writing assignments at the end of each unit in this book. These assignments allow students to synthesize and expand upon what they are studying in each unit.

You will need to decide how you will respond to student journal writing. Here are a few suggestions.

- Respond only to the content of what is written in the journal.

- Look for positive examples of vocabulary and grammar usage consistent with each chapter and highlight or underline them in student journals.

- Tell students you are going to read their journals with an eye toward a particular kind of writing: a descriptive sentence, an opinion, a comparison, an analysis or explanation, and so on. Then identify that writing when you come across it in student journals.

- Ask students to read something from their journals during class time. Ask the students listening to respond in writing to what they hear.

- Each week, read selected journal entries aloud to the entire class to inspire and foster respect among students for each other as writers.

Appendices   Each text contains appendices of grammar and writing conventions for student reference. During your first class meeting, when you familiarize students with the book, make sure you take some time to point out the appendices and what they contain. Students too often discover appendices at the end of a course.

Instructor's Edition   The Instructor's Edition of *From Paragraph to Essay* contains unit-by-unit notes of explanation, advice, suggestions, and reproducible tests for each unit.

Web Site   The *Writing to Learn* web site can be located through the McGraw-Hill, Inc. web site at <www.mhhe.com> This interactive site should be useful to instructors and students. For instructors, the site can be a virtual teacher's room, where instructors can raise questions and exchange ideas and activities related to this series. Students can post and read writing assignments for each unit and thus expand the walls of their classroom.

From Paragraph to Essay

This third book in the series emphasizes writing well-organized paragraphs in the first four units and writing essays in the last two units. Picture stories are used to elicit vocabulary, discussion, and student opinion. Writing assignments cover both vocational and academic topics. Student success in using this book should be based on ability to create a meaningful paragraph from the beginning step of brainstorming information to redrafting for style, grammaticality, effect on the reader, and content. So while one goal of the text is to expose students to the form of the English paragraph, another goal is to give them some thinking tools to use in creating their own paragraphs.

The First Lesson

Begin your first class with an exercise that helps your students become familiar with this text. You can do this orally, in writing, or both. Students might work in pairs or small groups. A familiarization exercise is contained in the *To the Student* part of the introduction to *From Paragraph to Essay*.

Question your students about the names of the six units, the number of sections in each unit, the number and names of the appendices, and their thoughts about the use of each unit section and appendix. Create and distribute a follow-up activity that reviews the text organization.

If you do the exercise orally, use the cooperative question-and-answer technique called "Numbered heads together." Have each student in a pair or group count off 1, 2 or 1, 2, 3, 4. Tell the class that before you call on anyone to answer, students who know the answer in a pair or group should tell the answer to their partner or group mates. Then pick a number. When you call "Number 1" for example, only students who are "Number 1" may raise their hands to answer. If the answer is correct, go on to the next question. If it is not, ask another "Number 1." In this way, you can begin teaching students to rely on their partners or group mates. We encourage students to turn to each other as resources for language learning. This is an essential element of process writing.

Acknowledgments

First and foremost, we acknowledge the debt of thanks we owe to our students at Santa Barbara City College, whose interests and concerns were the catalyst that led us to embark on this writing project. We would like to thank as well our colleagues at City College, especially Frank Lazorchik and Julie Alpert and others in the larger field of ESOL writing, who often made valuable suggestions to us about our manuscripts.

This book and this series would not have been written without the encouragement and persistence of Tim Stookesberry, Aurora Martínez, and Pam Tiberia at McGraw-Hill, and our series editor, the inimitable, indefatigable, and empathetic Bob Hemmer.

Should you have any suggestions or comments, we would be happy to receive them from you in writing, via email, or at our web site. You can write to us in care of the ESL Department, Santa Barbara City College, Santa Barbara, California, 93109, USA. Our email address is spaventa@sbcc.net.

Lou and Marilynn Spaventa
Santa Barbara, California

To the Student

Welcome to *From Paragraph to Essay!*

The goal of this book is to help you write good English paragraphs and essays. The book has six units. Each unit has a topic that you will discuss and write about. The topic for Unit One is Myself and Others. Look for the topics of the other units. Look in the Table of Contents. Write the names of the topics below.

Unit One   <u>Myself and Others</u>

Unit Two   _____

Unit Three   _____

Unit Four   _____

Unit Five   _____

Unit Six   _____

Take five minutes to skim (look quickly) through the units. Look only at the first page of each unit. Then close the book. Write down whatever words come into your mind. Write down words about what you saw.

_____

_____

_____

Each unit has four sections. Match the section with its description. Draw a line from the section to its description.

Section	Description
Prewriting	gives ideas for writing on your own in a journal
Structure	practices English grammar
Writing and Editing	prepares you for writing by learning vocabulary and giving ideas to discuss
Journal Assignment	has exercises to improve your writing skills

Your instructor will decide how to use this book in the best way for you. We designed *From Paragraph to Essay* as a workbook, so please write in it.

Now you have met our book *From Paragraph to Essay.* Your instructor may ask you some questions about the book. Be prepared to answer them. We hope you enjoy working with the book. Remember that learning to write well is a skill. You need to practice a skill to write well. Write a lot. Write what you feel and what you think. Learn a lot!

Lou and Marilynn Spaventa

Writing to Learn
FROM PARAGRAPH TO ESSAY

Myself and Others

A Prewriting

Exercise 1. Saying hello Move around the room, saying hello to your classmates. Greet them with a handshake, a gesture used by many people in the English-speaking world. Say hello to as many people as you can. You have five minutes.

Before you go back to your seat, write your first and last names on the board. Your teacher will begin this activity by asking, *"Who is Al Smith?"* If that is your name, you must stand up and say, *"I am Al Smith. I am from* (your country)." Then add one more piece of information to your greeting.

EXAMPLE: 1. I am Al Smith. I am from Canada. I speak French and English.

or

2. I am Al Smith. I am from Canada. I have a brother who is studying here.

Now take turns reading another name and asking the question, *"Who is (next student's name)?"* The exercise will continue until everyone has had a chance to stand up and say his or her name to the class.

Exercise 2. Greetings—the same and different Look at the pictures on page 3 of people greeting one another. Identify the type of greeting used in each picture. Make a list of countries and greetings that you know on page 4.

2

Unit 1: Myself and Others

Country	Greeting
The United States of America	handshake
Canada	handshake
Korea	bow

Now use your list to move around the classroom again. If your class has many people from different countries, ask each person how they greet one another in that country. If your class has students mostly from one country, compare your list of countries and greetings with your classmates.

Exercise 3. Brainstorming   Think about how many times you pick up a pencil or pen every day to write in your first language. How many different kinds of writing do you do? How many different kinds of writing are there?

Answer these questions in your group. One student in your group needs to write down what the others say. Everyone should give ideas. Do not worry about spelling. Do not write in complete sentences. Use words and phrases. Write as many ideas as your group can think of in five minutes.

When you finish, exchange your information with another group or with the whole class by reading your list aloud. Getting all of your ideas and sharing them is called *brainstorming.*

Notes

_____

_____

_____

_____

_____

_____

_____

_____

_____

_____

 Exercise 4. Brainstorming a greeting   Think of as many new ways to greet another person as you can. Practice them in your group. Consider these questions:

- How do men greet women?

- How do children greet adults?

- How do men greet men?

- How do women greet women?

- How do adults greet old people?

- How do children greet each other?

 Now create a new imaginary greeting for your group. Pretend your group members all come from the same country. First make up a name for your country and a name for the language that you speak. Then create a greeting. Make it different from the greetings you have already seen and heard about. Tell the class the name of your country and the name of the language that you speak. Show the rest of the class your greeting.

Exercise 5. Writing to communicate   Writing is an important way of communicating. For the next twenty minutes, write to as many classmates as possible. Don't forget that you can write to your teacher, too.

- write *short* notes

- introduce yourself, ask questions, give information

- sign your notes

- fold each note, then get up and deliver it

- answer the notes you receive

- don't worry about mistakes in grammar and spelling

There is only one important rule. *Do not talk at all!* Work fast. This should be fun! You will get writing practice and get to know your classmates at the same time.

EXAMPLES:

> Hi! What's your name? What country do you come from? You are so quiet. Are you shy?
>
> Mario

> I like the shirt you're wearing today.
>
> Svetlana

B   Structure

Exercise 1. Present time review

Uses of the Present Tense

To discuss things in present time, use the tenses below.

Tense → Time ↓	Present Simple	Present Continuous	Present Perfect	Present Perfect Continuous
Present	Lou *practices* guitar every day.	Right now, Lou is *not practicing* guitar. He's writing.	Lou *has written* a few books on teaching English.	Lou *has been playing* guitar for years.

Writing to Learn: *From Paragraph to Essay*

The examples in the chart do not include all uses for each tense in present time. Each tense has more than one use. Here are some uses of the present simple tense.

1. Expressing things that happen regularly

   EXAMPLE: Lou plays guitar every day.

2. Expressing things that never change

   EXAMPLE: The sun sets in the west.

3. Labeling things with the verb **be**

   EXAMPLE: Marilynn is an ESL instructor.

4. Expressing future time with future time adverb

   EXAMPLE: Prof. Bing lectures at 8 P.M. tomorrow.

Write the number (1–4 from the list above) of the use of the present tense that corresponds to each sentence that follows.

   EXAMPLE: __2__   The sun rises in the east.

_____ a. John works out in the gym daily.

_____ b. Kate never forgets her homework.

_____ c. Peter leaves for New York next week.

_____ d. Alex is a jazz pianist.

_____ e. Your book bag is old and worn.

_____ f. Water boils at 100° centigrade.

Think about the other three present tenses mentioned earlier. Write two sentences for each of them. Make the sentences different in meaning.

Present Continuous

1. _____

2. _____

Present Perfect

3. _____

4. _____

Present Perfect Continuous

5. _____

6. _____

Exercise 2. Past time review

Uses of the Past Tense

To discuss things in past time, use the tenses below.

Tense → Time ↓	Past Simple	Past* Continuous	Past* Perfect	Past* Perfect Continuous
Present	Lou *practiced* guitar yesterday.	Lou was practicing guitar when I got home.	Lou *had written* a play before he wrote a novel.	Lou *had been playing* guitar for years when he stopped.

*Notice that these tenses do not occur alone, but as part of complex sentences. Here they are part of the independent clause in each sentence.

The examples in the chart include only a few of the different uses for each tense in past time. Each tense has more than one use. Here are some uses of the past simple tense.

1. Describing something that happened in the past

   EXAMPLE: Louisa graduated from college five years ago.

2. Describing a past habit or repeated action

   EXAMPLE: It rained almost that whole winter.

3. Describing conditions in the past

   EXAMPLE: She owed her parents over $10,000.

4. Describing something true in the past but not in the present (*used to* + verb can give the same meaning).

   EXAMPLE: People traveled long distances by steam engine.

Write the number (1–4 from the list on page 8) of each use of the past tense that corresponds to each sentence that follows.

EXAMPLE: __2__ He drove his son to school every day.

_____ a. Last year John worked out in the gym daily.

_____ b. Kate had insomnia for a number of years.

_____ c. Peter left for New York last week.

_____ d. Alex was a jazz pianist.

_____ e. A thief took your book bag.

_____ f. Every town in colonial America had a blacksmith.

Think about the other three past tenses mentioned earlier. Write two sentences for each of them. Make the sentences different in meaning.

Past Continuous

1. _____

2. _____

Past Perfect

3. _____

4. _____

Past Perfect Continuous

5. _____

6. _____

Exercise 3. Uniformity in tense When you write, you should be consistent in your use of tense. When you refer to the past, use the past tense consistently. When you refer to the present, use the present tense consistently. The paragraph on page 10 has errors in verb tenses. Find the errors and correct them.

An Outdoor Person

Gail is a person who loves to be outdoors. She is very athletic and she skied a lot. Every winter she went to her uncle's house in the mountains where she skis. Skiing is not her only outdoor interest. Gail also loved to run and play tennis. However, a couple of years ago, she has a knee operation. Because of this, she stopped running marathons for a while. These days she has been running marathons again. Her knee is much better, and she also could play tennis daily. She lived in California for ten years. California is the perfect place for her because the sun always shined and the weather is always warm, and there was snow in the nearby mountains in winter.

Exercise 4: More uniformity in tense   In this story, there are several errors in verb tense. Read the story and change the verbs that you need to.

Irma and Hilario

Irma and Hilario living in the United States for the past six months. Irma was twenty-one years old. She studies English every night in an adult education program. Her brother Hilario studied, too. Irma and Hilario come from Zacatecas, Mexico. Their parents still live there, but all their brothers and sisters living in the United States. Irma likes to write in English, but Hilario didn't. He prefers just learning to speak better. Now he worked as a gardener for a big landscaping company. Hilario says that he just needs to speak and understand English. Irma did not agree with Hilario. She thinks writing is important. She wanted to study English and enter a university in the future. Hilario enjoys working as a gardener. He wants to start his own business one day.

Writing to Learn: *From Paragraph to Essay*

Verb Plus Verb

In English, when two verbs are used in combination, the first verb shows the tense and the second verb must be either an infinitive or the gerund form. The first verb determines the form of the second verb. There is no rule to help you; you must memorize the combinations.

> **EXAMPLE:** I want to learn English.
>
> I enjoy learning English.

Some verbs allow the second verb to take either the infinitive or the gerund form. There is usually a small difference in meaning, and in a few instances the difference is very big.

> **EXAMPLE:** I like learning English. *(The emphasis here is on the process of learning.)*
>
> I like to learn English. *(The emphasis here is on the fact of learning.)*

Here are some common verbs you may need for your writing assignments. There are many more to add to this list. Many grammar books contain extensive lists of these verbs.

Verbs that take the -ing gerund form	Verbs that take the to infinitive form	Verbs that take either form with small difference in meaning	Verbs that take either form with very different meanings
appreciate	ask	begin	forget
discuss	come	continue	remember
dislike	decide	hate	stop
don't mind	hope	like	try
enjoy	learn	love	
feel like	need	plan	
finish	promise	prefer	
miss	want	start	
quit	wish		
suggest	would like to		

Exercise 5. Verb plus verb   Use the verbs that follow to write sentences about yourself. The first verb can be in any tense. The second verb must be an infinitive or gerund. Refer to the chart on page 11 for help.

EXAMPLE: enjoy, attend
I enjoy attending class because I meet a lot of new people.

1. finish, do

_____

2. suggest, go

_____

3. hope, learn

_____

4. want, visit

_____

5. hate, see

_____

6. love, eat

_____

7. don't mind, work

_____

8. continue, study

_____

9. started, walk

_____

10. decide, buy

_____

Writing to Learn: *From Paragraph to Essay*

Exercise 6. Interviewing a partner   Use your sentences from Exercise 5 to ask questions of your partner. Make notes about what your partner tells you.

EXAMPLE: I love to eat French fries. How about you? Do you love to eat them, too?

Notes

_____

_____

_____

_____

_____

_____

_____

_____

_____

_____

Now form a group with another pair of students. Introduce your partner to the group by reporting on what he or she said to you in answer to your questions.

Exercise 7. More verb-plus-verb practice   Here is a list of common activities. Write ten sentences about yourself using these words and the list of verbs on page 11.

EXAMPLES: I usually enjoy driving in the country.

I like cooking dinner for my family.

cooking	dancing	to take a nap	driving
to write	to get married	cleaning	to study
commuting	walking	to talk	reading
to teach	learning	to travel	making money

1. _____

2. _____

3. _____

4. _____

5. _____

6. _____

7. _____

8. _____

9. _____

10. _____

Exercise 8. Pronoun review   Read the story about Yuko Takai two times. Read for comprehension the first time and talk with your partner about how you are similar to or different from Yuko. Then, read the story a second time and circle all of the pronouns.

Someone Like Me

I left my hometown, Osaka, last year. I arrived in Los Angeles in the spring. The weather was beautiful, but I felt very nervous. I was alone in a new place. I came to the United States to study English. I wanted to get away from Osaka. All my friends told me I was foolish. My friends worked in good companies. I had worked in a good company, too, but I quit my job. I did not like my life because it was not interesting or exciting.

I started studying here last semester. Before studying here, I had studied in Los Angeles. In L.A., I did not speak much English, and I didn't learn much English. I hung out in Little Tokyo. I ate in Japanese restaurants. I went to a Japanese hair stylist. I bought the Japanese

---

newspaper. I made friends, but they were all Japanese. None of them was like me. All of them wanted to return to Japan and get good jobs.

I left L.A. last summer, and now I live here. I don't have many Japanese friends, but I do speak and understand English better. I have made two friends who speak Spanish. One of them is like me. She gave up a good job to try something different. She wants to be a translator. The other friend is from Barcelona. He is an artist. I showed him some of my drawings. He thinks that I have talent. Both of my new friends want to change their lives.

Pronouns

In English, pronouns are used in place of nouns, especially when the noun is repeated often in a paragraph.

EXAMPLES: Yuko left L.A. last summer, and now **she** lives here. **She** doesn't have many Japanese friends, but **she** does understand and speak English better.

As the paragraph continues, the writer has to decide when to use pronouns and when to use the nouns that they stand for.

EXAMPLES: **She** has made two friends who speak Spanish. One of **them** is like **her. Her** friend gave up a good job to try something different. **She** wants to be a translator. The other friend is from Barcelona. **He** is an artist. Yuko showed **him** some of **her** drawings. **He** thinks that **she** has talent. Both of Yuko's friends want to change **their** lives.

Now, rewrite the first part of the story from the third person perspective. Put in pronouns where you think they should go. Remember to use both nouns and pronouns to make your story interesting. See page 158 for a reference chart on pronouns.

Yuko left Yuko's hometown, Osaka, last year. Yuko arrived in Los Angeles in the spring. The weather was beautiful, but Yuko felt very nervous. Yuko was alone in a new place. Yuko came to the United States to study English. Yuko wanted to get away from Osaka. All Yuko's friends told Yuko Yuko was foolish. Yuko's friends worked in good companies. Yuko had worked in a good company, too, but Yuko quit Yuko's job. Yuko did not like Yuko's life because Yuko's life was not interesting or exciting.

Yuko started studying here last semester. Before studying here, Yuko had studied in Los Angeles. In L.A., Yuko did not speak much English, and Yuko didn't learn much English. Yuko hung out in Little Tokyo. Yuko ate in Japanese restaurants. Yuko went to a Japanese hair stylist. Yuko bought the Japanese newspaper. Yuko made friends, but Yuko's friends were all Japanese. None of Yuko's friends was like Yuko. All of Yuko's friends wanted to return to Japan and get good jobs.

_____

_____

_____

_____

_____

_____

_____

_____

_____

_____

_____

_____

_____

_____

_____

_____

_____

_____

_____

Exercise 9. Writing a paragraph about yourself   How is Yuko similar to you? How is she different from you? Write a paragraph with one of these titles: "I Am Like Yuko" or "I Am Different from Yuko."

_____

_____

_____

_____

_____

_____

_____

_____

```
_____

_____

_____

_____

_____

_____

_____

_____
```

C   Writing and Editing

Exercise 1. Organizing notes   After you brainstorm or make notes for a paragraph, you have to decide on your focus, or main idea. Sometimes you have to cut or delete some information. For example, if you are writing only one paragraph about someone, you cannot write that person's whole life story.

Look at these notes for a paragraph about a student named Daniel. Make groups of related information. One way you can do this is by using numbers to code similar ideas.

Use numbers to organize the following information in a more focused way. Some notes are already numbered as an example.

Daniel

___1___ born in 1973

_____ hardworking

_____ goal = accountant

___3___ likes basketball

_____ enjoys writing letters to his family

___1___ mother died in 1980

_____ five siblings live in Mexico

_____ serious

___2___ attended one year of university in Mexico City

___1___ eight brothers and sisters

___3___ athletic

_____ likes dancing

Writing to Learn: *From Paragraph to Essay*

___2___ studied French for one year

_____ three brothers live in the United States

_____ wants to marry his girlfriend soon

_____ brother helping him with money now

_____ family gets together every summer

How many possible paragraphs could you write about Daniel? _____

 Exercise 2. Limiting the topic by grouping   Look at these notes about an ESL teacher. Group the related ideas. Cross out any notes that are not related. Practice two methods of organizing. First, group by writing categories in the chart that follows. Because there are different ways of thinking, it is possible for you to put an idea in a different category than your classmate does. Both ways can be right. Some of the notes may not fit into any category.

Gail

loves teaching people from other countries

friends and family are very important for her

loves to ski, plays tennis

has visited twenty countries

went to high school in Pasadena, California

likes to spend vacation traveling

went to a small college in New York/liked it but too cold

Got a "D" in a course because she went to a political protest instead of the final exam

doesn't attend a traditional church

loved art and theater in college

didn't like to study in college

has run in several marathons

transferred from a college in New York to UCLA

isn't married/no children

went to France for one semester in college

swam in college but didn't do any sports

was interested in politics in college

attended graduate school in Vermont with students from all over the world

loves challenge and adventure

loves her family

likes to spend holidays with family

wants to go to Africa

loves cats

Gail's Pastimes and Interests	Gail's Education	Gail's International Interests

Now organize the same information in the following map.

Writing to Learn: *From Paragraph to Essay*

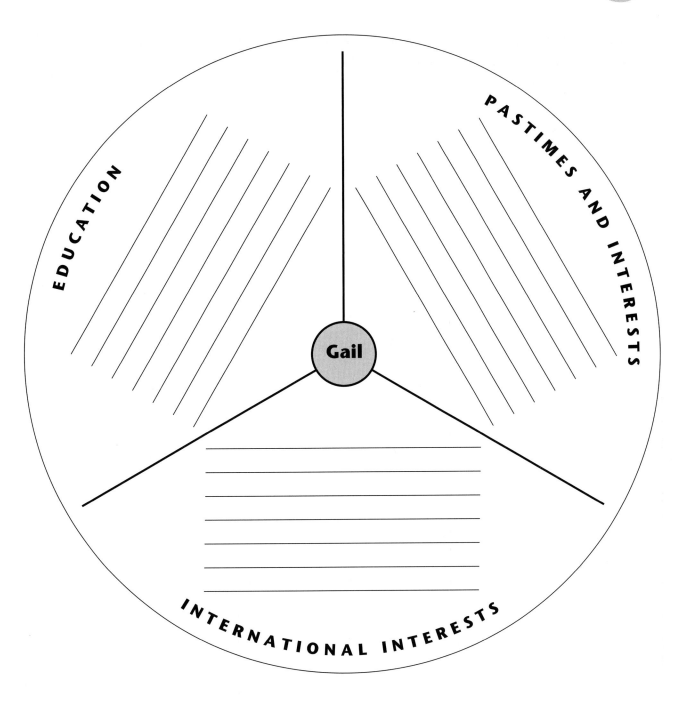

 You have practiced three different methods of organizing before writing. Which do you prefer? Why?

Exercise 3. Writing a topic sentence   When you write a paragraph or an essay, you need to have a main idea or *point of view*. That is the *focus*. A *topic sentence* is the sentence in the paragraph that gives the main idea or the writer's point of view. It often comes at the beginning of the paragraph. A topic sentence should also be interesting.

 Notice that the topic sentence is part of a paragraph. It is usually not a separate paragraph.

   EXAMPLE: Incorrect

Josue's Success

Josue accomplished his goals in the ESL program.

He completed all five levels and got good grades. In fact, he was one of the best. In addition to doing well in classes, he was very popular. He

〰〰〰〰〰〰〰〰〰〰〰〰〰〰〰〰

〰〰〰〰〰〰〰〰〰〰〰〰〰〰〰〰

〰〰〰〰〰〰〰〰〰〰〰〰〰〰〰〰

   EXAMPLE: Correct

Josue's Success

   Josue accomplished his goals in the ESL program. He completed all five levels and got good grades. In fact, he was one of the best students in his grammar class. In addition to doing well in classes, he was very popular. He was well liked by his teachers and his classmates. He even tutored some of his classmates in grammar. His greatest success was when he was selected student of the year for the ESL department in 1999.

Read the following paragraph about an ESL teacher. Write a topic sentence for it.

_____. His first experience in another country was on a beautiful island south of Korea. It was such a wonderful experience that he decided to live and work in other parts of the world, too. As a graduate student, he lived and worked in Mexico. He taught in Saudi Arabia next. Everything about his life was different there. Then he went back to Korea, but this time to the capital city, Seoul. After that, he lived in Hawaii. Although Hawaii is part of the United States, it is very different from New York, where he grew up. His travels continued to Yugoslavia, England, and Barbados. Now he's teaching me here. I wonder where he will go next.

Exercise 4. Staying with the topic When you write a paragraph, be sure that all of the ideas and sentences are focused or related to the topic sentence, or controlling sentence. Read this paragraph. Circle the topic sentence. Cross out the sentence that does not belong in this paragraph.

Carlo and His Camera

Carlo has always wanted to be a professional photographer. He got his first camera for his seventh birthday. When he was in high school, he took photographs for the school newspaper. Although he takes pictures of everything, he especially likes to photograph people. He speaks two languages besides Italian. Carlo plans to study photography at Brooks Photography Institute after his English improves. His dream is to publish a book of photographs of famous people.

Read the following paragraph. Rewrite it, putting the sentences in the best order. Underline the topic sentence, or controlling idea. One sentence is not related to the controlling idea. Do not include it.

An Actor in the Making

He studied acting for two years in France. He's a very handsome man, so I can imagine him starring in a romantic movie. He thinks the United States is a wonderful place for anyone to live. He knows that he must first improve his speaking and listening ability in English, so he likes to practice pronunciation and listening in the language laboratory. Now he wants to try acting in a new language. François wants to take acting classes after he finishes the ESL program. He loves it when we do class activities that require conversations for role play.

_____

_____

_____

_____

_____

_____

_____

_____

_____

_____

_____

Exercise 5. Writing in paragraph form   The form of a paragraph is important. (See Appendix VIII on page 167).

- Center the title and use correct form.
- Indent about one-half inch at the beginning of a paragraph. If you are using a computer, use the tab key to indent.
- One sentence follows another in a paragraph. Leave a little space after each sentence. If you are using a computer, leave two spaces. If you are using a computer, do not use the return or enter key.

Write the following title and sentences in paragraph form.

lovely Damaris

Damaris is one of my nicest classmates.

She always has a smile on her face and a kind word.

She learns everybody's name quickly and always remembers to greet each person.

Damaris usually sits in front of the class so that she can concentrate.

Maybe she likes to sit there to smile at the teacher, too.

_____

_____

_____

_____

_____

_____

_____

 Exercise 6. Editing titles   Write the following titles with correct capitalization and punctuation.

        EXAMPLE: welcome to my class
               Welcome to My Class

Titles

Frequently, titles are not complete sentences in English. When you write titles in English, follow these rules.

- Capitalize the first word.
- Capitalize all words except articles (**a, an, the,** etc.) and prepositions (**to, from at,** etc.) Pronouns are usually capitalized.
- Remember that countries, languages, and people from countries are always capitalized (American, French, Korean, etc.)
- Do not use a period (.) at the end, but you may need a question mark (?) or an exclamation mark (!).
- Center a title.

  EXAMPLES: Meet Takahiro

  The Amazing Alfredo!

  A Student with a Dream

1. the girl from costa rica

   _____

2. gloria's goal

   _____

3. a hardworking young man from guatemala

   _____

4. a man with big plans

   _____

5. alone but not lonely

   _____

6. susie's surprise

   _____

7. shy or respectful

   _____

8. from taiwan to chicago

   _____

9. a new life in vancouver

   _____

10. keiko loves new york

    _____

Exercise 7. Writing titles   Like a topic sentence, the title tells the reader your focus. Do not forget that a title should be interesting, too. You want to get your reader's attention even before he or she begins to read your paragraph or essay. As a writer, writing a title can help you focus, too.

Read this paragraph, and then choose the best title from the list that follows.

> _____
>
> Luis likes to study, but he loves to play soccer. When he was a boy, his father always told him, "Study hard and get a good education." Luis listened to his father. He always studied hard and got good grades, but he was happier when he was kicking a soccer ball around the field. Now his father is very proud of him because he is a student at City College. Luis plays on the college soccer team, too. He is happy because he can do both of the things he loves.

Which is the best title? (Which title shows the **focus** of the paragraph?) Why? Write the title in the space provided.

1. Luis Comes from Argentina

2. Luis

3. A Student and a Soccer Player

4. Study Hard! Play Hard!

Now read the following paragraph. After you have read it, write a title for it.

_____

When you first see Takahiro, you think he is a typical student. This is only half true. Takahiro is a student, but he is not typical. In fact, I was very surprised when I talked to him. Takahiro was in the army in his country. He was a special forces soldier and a judo expert. He liked his life in the army, but he wanted a change. Now he is a student at City College. When you see Takahiro, talk to him. Everyone will want to be his friend. Maybe everybody will be a little afraid of him, too!

Now compare your title with your classmates' titles.

Exercise 8. Revising your writing Read the following first draft of a student's paragraph and answer the questions.

First Draft

J o s e

Jose is Peruvian.

He looks healthy and active, and his hobby is fishing for baby sharks. He goes fishing once a month. He likes dancing and drinking. His favorite drink is beer.

My first impression of him is that he is a gentleman because he speaks clearly.

1. How many paragraphs are there?   _____

2. Is the title interesting?   _____

3. What are the controlling ideas?

_____

_____

Read the following second draft and answer the questions.

Second Draft

J o s e

Jose looks healthy and active.

His hobby is fishing baby sharks. He liked fishing when he was a little boy in Peru. He used to go fishing with his father and his brothers. He has a lot of brothers and sisters. He misses his family. He can't go fishing with his family now because he has been living here alone for three years. Now, he goes fishing once a month with his friends or alone.

Sometimes he goes to a disco downtown. He likes dancing and drinking, and his favorite drink is beer. I think that he is a heavy drinker.

---

1. How many paragraphs are there?   _____

2. Is the title interesting?   _____

3. What are the controlling ideas?

_____

_____

4. Which idea is most interesting to you?

_____

_____

Read the following third draft and answer the questions.

Third Draft

Jose the Fisherman

Jose loves fishing. His hobby is fishing for baby sharks. He liked fishing when he was a little boy in Peru. He used to go fishing with his father and his brothers. He can't go fishing with his family now because he lives here. Now he goes fishing once a month with his friends. Sometimes he fishes alone. I would like to go fishing with him some day!

---

1. How many paragraphs are there?   _____

2. Is the title more interesting?   _____

3. Does the title give you the main
   idea of the paragraph?   _____

4. Underline the topic sentence. Are
   all of the sentences related to the
   controlling idea?   _____

5. What ideas did the writer cut?

   _____

   _____

   _____

Exercise 9. Writing assignment: writing about a classmate

Step 1. Find a partner you don't know. Write twenty interesting questions to ask that person.

1. _____

2. _____

3. _____

4. _____

5. _____

6. _____

7. _____

8. _____

9. _____

10. _____

11. _____

12. _____

13. _____

14. _____

15. _____

16. _____

17. _____

18. _____

19. _____

20. _____

 Step 2. Spend twenty minutes together. Introduce yourself. Your partner can ask you his or her questions. Then your partner can introduce himself or herself, and you can ask your questions. When you find out something interesting, ask additional questions on that topic to find out more details. Do not write anything during the interview.

Step 3. In five minutes, write down everything that you can remember about your partner. Don't write in complete sentences. Don't worry about mistakes.

Notes

_____

_____

_____

_____

_____

_____

_____

_____

_____

_____

_____

_____

_____

_____

 Step 4. Meet with your partner again. Your partner should read what you wrote and can make corrections about information. You can ask more questions.

Step 5. Organize your notes in a chart or map.

Step 6. Find a focus or main idea. You cannot write your partner's life story in one paragraph! Write the focus in a few words.

    EXAMPLE: Takahiro is not the way he looks.

Step 7. Write a title and topic sentence.

_____

_____

_____

Step 8. Write a paragraph about your partner.

Exercise 10. Revising assignment

Step 1. You and your partner need to work with another pair. Exchange your paragraphs with your new partners.

Step 2. Read the paragraph from your new partner. Underline the topic sentence.

Step 3. Make sure that all the sentences are related to the topic sentence. If there is a sentence that is not related, ask your partner to explain why it is in the paragraph. Maybe she or he will want to cut it.

Step 4. If you need or want to make changes in your paragraph, rewrite it.

D Journal Assignment

Choose one topic to write about in your journal for each class, or as your teacher assigns you. Before writing, be sure to read about journal writing in the appendix on page 169.

- My first day in this country
- It isn't easy being me
- One thing I don't like about myself
- One thing I don't like about my life
- One thing I would never change about myself
- How I want my children to be like me
- How I want my children to be different from me
- What I want to find out about X's (name of a classmate) culture
- What I know about X's (name of a classmate) culture
- A person in this class I would like to get to know better and why

Complete the personal information section from a sample employment application. Other sections are found in the journal writing part of Units Three and Four. See Appendix XII on pages 171–173 for a complete sample application.

Personal

(Please use blue or black ink and print clearly.)

Name _____
    first name   middle initial   last name

*Social Security Number _____

Street Address _____ Apt. No. or Box _____

City _____ State _____ Zip Code _____

Telephone Number _____

Are you 18 or older?   ☐ Yes   ☐ No

*Please note a social security number is required to work in the United States.

Family and Relationships

A Prewriting

1.

2.

3.

4.

Exercise 1. Making connections   Each person in your group chooses one of the pictures in the picture story and writes as many words as possible on the picture for three minutes. Then, each person explains the vocabulary for his/her picture.

Look at the four pictures again. What connections can you find? Develop a group story. One person should write down the group's ideas.

Put your papers away. Find a partner from a different group. Tell your partner what your group said about the picture story.

Exercise 2. Writing a story   Write a story for the four pictures on page 38. You can write your group's story, the story from another group, or a new story. Add as many details as possible. Be sure to give names to all of the characters in your story.

_____

_____

_____

_____

_____

_____

_____

_____

_____

_____

_____

_____

_____

_____

_____

_____

_____

_____

_____

_____

_____

Exercise 3. Freewriting *Freewriting* is an exercise designed to improve fluency and spontaneity in your writing. The main idea is to write as much as possible. Put your pen on the paper and write. Do not think about spelling, punctuation, or grammar. Just keep writing the whole time, even if you write off the topic.

The topic is *family*. For five minutes, write as much as you can. In English, write everything and anything that comes into your mind. Do not worry about mistakes. Do not edit your writing by crossing out or erasing.

Family

_____

_____

_____

_____

_____

_____

_____

_____

_____

_____

_____

_____

_____

_____

_____

_____

_____

_____

_____

_____

Writing to Learn: *From Paragraph to Essay*

Read your writing to the people in your group. Do not show it to them. Just read it as clearly as you can. You can stop to explain more or answer a question as you read.

Exercise 4. Relationship vocabulary   What do you call the following people?

EXAMPLE: your mother's brother   _____my uncle_____

1. your father's brother   _____

2. your mother's mother   _____

3. your mother's sister's son   _____

4. your father's brother's daughter   _____

5. your mother's sister   _____

6. your father's mother and father   _____

7. your father's father's father   _____

8. your sister's son   _____

9. your brother's son   _____

10. your sister's daughter   _____

11. your wife's (husband's) family   _____

12. your wife's (husband's) sister   _____

13. your father's new wife   _____

14. _____   _____
       (your question)

Exercise 5. Identifying family members   Think about your own family. Write sentences about the members of your family on page 42. First write a sentence to explain what relationship that person has to you. Then write another sentence with additional information.

Unit 2: Family and Relationships

41

Name and relationship	Additional information
John is my brother.	He loves to play basketball.

Exercise 6. Talking about family   Bring a picture of your family or of someone in your family to class. Prepare to talk from three to five minutes about the picture to your classmates. After everyone talks, write notes to each other to ask for more information about the family or family member. Answer the questions, and pass the notes back.

Exercise 7. Interactions   Think about how you interact with your family members. What do you do together? What sort of things do you say to each other? Write a sentence or sentences for each family member that you mentioned in Exercises 5 and 6.

EXAMPLES: I play checkers with my brother Antonio.

My mother usually tells me to do things, like clean my room.

_____

_____

_____

Writing to Learn: *From Paragraph to Essay*

_____

_____

_____

_____

_____

_____

_____

B Structure

Exercise 1. Combining sentences with *and, but, so,* and *or* An easy way to combine sentences is to use the coordinating conjunctions **and, but, so,** and **or.** Underline each subject once and each verb twice in the sentences in the three examples that follow. See Appendix I on page 157 for more information on subjects and verbs.

Coordinating Conjunctions and Independent Clauses

EXAMPLE: Subject + Verb + Object **and, but, so, or** Subject + Verb + Object

My <u>family</u> <u>speaks</u> Spanish, and <u>I</u> <u>speak</u> Spanish, too (and I do, too/so do I).

1. My father speaks English, **but** my mother doesn't (speak English).

2. My mother stays home, **so** she doesn't have the opportunity to learn.

3. My brother may study here, **or** he may go to Los Angeles.*

* Notice that even when the subject is the same in both clauses, you need a subject in the second clause.

These conjunctions are called *coordinating conjunctions*. They all work the same way, but they have different meanings.

and = addition   **so** = result

but = contrast   **or** = choice

(Continued)

Coordinating conjunctions combine two *independent clauses.* An independent clause has a subject and verb. It is a complete sentence in itself.

EXAMPLE: My grandfather speaks Turkish and Albanian.

I speak only Albanian.

Coordinating conjunctions combine two independent clauses into one sentence.

EXAMPLE: My grandfather speaks Turkish and Albanian, **but** I speak only Albanian.

When you combine two sentences into one sentence using these words, remember to put a comma after the last word in the first sentence.

Circle the two independent clauses in the preceding example sentence.

 Exercise 2. Choosing the correct coordinating conjunction Write a comma and a coordinating conjunction for each of the following sentences. Use the chart on page 45 for help.

EXAMPLE: My mother works hard, _____but_____ she also has time for us.

1. My uncle is the president of a large company _____ he earns a lot of money.

2. My cousin is married _____ he has five children.

3. My sister is only sixteen _____ she isn't married yet.

4. My great-grandmother is ninety-eight years old _____ she still enjoys good health.

5. My brother-in-law has just arrived in this country _____ he needs to learn English.

6. My husband works hard _____ he always has time to read to the children.

7. My boyfriend recently asked me to marry him _____ I said yes.

8. She is living with her fiancé _____ her mother doesn't know it.

9. My cousin may fly to New York for Christmas _____ he may come visit me in London.

10. I have to drive to Vancouver _____ I have to fly stand-by. (There are no plane tickets left.)

Writing to Learn: *From Paragraph to Essay*

Sentence Combining Chart

Relationship	Two independent clauses
addition	**, and** I can sing well, **and** I can play the guitar like a professional.
contrast	**, but** I studied hard, **but** I failed the test.
cause and effect	**, so** It rained, **so** the picnic was cancelled.
choice	**, or** You can pay now, **or** you pay later.

Exercise 3. More sentence combining Combine the sentences, using one of the coordinating conjunctions.

EXAMPLE: My brother will emigrate to Canada. My uncle will emigrate to Australia.
My brother will emigrate to Canada, and my uncle will emigrate to Australia.

1. My Uncle Pedro plays guitar well. My Uncle Pedro doesn't play piano.

_____

2. Next summer I may visit my family. Next summer my family may visit me.

_____

3. My sister's fiancé has a good job. My sister's fiancé can afford to buy a new car.

_____

4. My grandmother died last year. My grandmother lived a full life.

_____

5. All of my cousins live in Texas. My aunts and my uncles live in Texas.

   _____

6. Jane wants to study music. Jane is applying to the New England Conservatory of Music.

   _____

7. My mother loves warm weather. My father dislikes warm weather.

   _____

8. (This school offers two foreign languages, French and Spanish) You can study French. You can study Spanish.

   _____

9. I sometimes drink coffee black. I sometimes drink coffee with cream and sugar.

   _____

10. My ex-mother-in-law* eats chicken. My ex-mother-in-law does not eat beef.

    _____

*ex- in front of a noun indicates a past relationship. In this case, the writer no longer legally has the same mother-in-law.

 Exercise 4. Reducing identical elements in combined sentences Look at your answers to Exercise 3. Underline identical words in the combined sentences. After you underline the identical words, omit the second identical word or words. Then recombine the sentences. Do not use a comma to separate the sentences.

EXAMPLE 1: <u>I don't</u> drink much tea, and <u>I don't</u> eat much meat.

I don't drink much tea and don't eat much meat.

EXAMPLE 2: <u>Peter often gets</u> As in English, but <u>Peter often gets</u> Ds in French.

Peter often gets As in English but Ds in French.

EXAMPLE 3: <u>Mary is working part-time</u> in the bookstore, and <u>Mary is working part-time</u> at the library.

Mary is working part-time in the bookstore and at the library.

1. _____

2. _____

3. _____

4. _____

5. _____

6. _____

7. _____

8. _____

9. _____

10. _____

Compare your answers with a partner.

Exercise 5. Revisiting the picture story   Reread what you wrote about the picture story in Exercise 2 on page 39. Combine whatever sentences you can by using coordinating conjunctions.

> **EXAMPLE:**   The old man in the park has a big nose. The man sitting at the table has a big nose.
>
> The old man in the park has a big nose, and the man sitting at the table has a big nose.

1. _____

2. _____

3. _____

4. _____

5. _____

6. _____

7. _____

8. _____

9. _____

10. _____

C Writing and Editing

Exercise 1. Using commas in a series

The Comma

Use commas to separate words or phrases that are in a series.

EXAMPLES: I am taller than my mother, my father, and my uncle.

I play tennis, swim, and write stories.

Do you come from Mexico, Guatemala, or El Salvador?

The comma before **and** or **or** is optional. The sentence can be written either way.

EXAMPLE: I am taller than my mother, my father, and my uncle.

I am taller than my mother, my father and my uncle.

Notice that the comma comes *immediately* after the word or phrase. There is no space between the word and the following comma. There is one space after the comma (• = 1 space).

Right: *I•am•taller•than•my•mother,•my•father,•and•my•uncle.*

Wrong: *I•am•taller•than•my•mother,•my•father•,•and•my•uncle.*

When **and** is used to combine only two words or phrases, English usually does not use a comma.

EXAMPLE: Who is taller, your mother or your father?

I got up and took a shower.

When you use the pronoun **I** or **me** in a series, it should be last, not first.

EXAMPLE: My brother, my sister and I are all short.

For the following sentences, decide whether to use commas to separate words. If you decide to use commas, then put them in the correct blank space.

EXAMPLE: Jose is a son__ __a husband__ __a father__ __and a brother.

Jose is a son, __a husband, __a father, __and a brother.

1. I have lived in a small village__ __and a big city.

2. My mother hurt her leg__ __her arm__ __and her face in the accident.

3. Have you been to Dallas__ __Pittsburgh__ __or Chicago?

4. My sister plans to finish ESL classes__ __get a nursing degree__ __and help support our mother.

5. Squash__ __spinach__ __broccoli__ __and brussel sprouts are not my kids' favorite vegetables, but I like them.

6. Tennis__ __swimming__ __and basketball are my sister's favorite activities.

7. My uncle can sing traditional folk songs__ __and popular songs.

8. Julie__ __Sara__ __and Andrew are all under ten years old.

9. My parents__ __my brother__ __my sister__ __and I have red hair.

10. Do you have a large extended family__ __or a small nuclear family?

Exercise 2. Writing about your family   Look back at Exercise 5 on pages 41–42. Write new sentences using that information together with new ideas. Write five combined sentences.

EXAMPLE: My brother loves to work out.

My son dislikes exercising.

My brother loves to work out, but my son dislikes exercising.

1. _____

2. _____

3. _____

4. _____

5. _____

Share your sentences with your group.

Exercise 3. Editing for punctuation Listen to your instructor read this paragraph out loud. Then read it again silently. This time, add commas and periods where necessary.

My Grandmother's Family

My grandmother is the most important person in our entire family so I always tell people that we are "Grandmother's family" My grandfather died twenty years ago but Grandmother was already the boss in the family She had always managed the money made the important decisions and arranged the marriages My grandmother is strong but she is gentle too She listens to secrets and she always gives good advice I love admire and respect my grandmother I hope that my children grow up to be as strong and honest as she is

 Exercise 4. Editing a story with coordinating conjunctions Read the story once all the way through. Then think about the relationship between events in the story. Combine sentences when you can. You may need to change nouns to pronouns when you combine. Use the coordinating conjunctions **and, but, so, and or.** If you know other words to use, you can try using them as well. Remember two things:

- There are many ways to do this exercise correctly.
- A good writer uses a variety of sentences, some simple and short, others combined and long.

Juan's Dream

Juan Garza left his family in Durango. He took a bus to Texas. He was nineteen years old. He was the third of six children. He had one hundred dollars in his pocket. Juan had a dream. He wanted to make money to send home to his family. He wanted to buy his mother a new house in Durango.

Juan found a job in a factory. He worked very hard. He worked long hours. Juan kept a picture of his family in his wallet. He looked at the picture whenever he felt homesick. He wanted to see his family. He didn't want to spend money on a ticket to Durango. Sometimes he wanted to quit his job. He didn't.

Juan began to study English. He got a better job. He started to save money. After three years, he had sent his mother a lot of money. His mother bought some land in the country. She started to build a new house for the family. Juan was happy.

Juan met a young woman from Texas. She didn't speak Spanish. They spoke in English. Juan was not homesick anymore. He began to have a new dream.

Exercise 5. Choosing conclusions   A title introduces your topic and gets your reader's attention. A topic sentence contains the controlling idea for your paragraph. A concluding sentence *closes* your paragraph.
Read the following paragraph. What is the controlling idea of the paragraph that appears in the title and the topic sentence?

_____

A Very Good Man

My father was a very good man. He wasn't rich or famous. He showed me how important it is to be a good person. Honesty and sincerity were the most important values he taught us. He always said, "Always tell the truth and you will always be happy with yourself." My father died when I was sixteen, but I still remember his advice. _____
[concluding sentence]

_____

There are several ways to write a concluding sentence. Here are some examples for this paragraph.

- You can summarize your controlling idea:
  EXAMPLE: For me, he was the perfect daddy.

- You can *mirror* the title or topic sentence.
  EXAMPLE: I will always remember him as a very good man.

Exercise 6. Writing concluding sentences Write a concluding sentence for the following paragraph. As a class, write all of the conclusions on the board. Choose which ones you like best.

Tears of Happiness

When I think about how we came to the United States, I always think of tears. We left our village at night so that nobody could see us. My mother was the only one who cried that night. After a dangerous journey, we arrived in a refugee camp in Thailand. We expected to stay there a short time, but we lived there for two years. I hated it there, but I never showed my feelings to my mother. Finally, we came to the United States. My father's brother and his family lived in Virginia. They were at the airport to meet us. We all cried when we got off the airplane. _____

_____

_____

Exercise 7. Avoiding new ideas in conclusions Remember that a paragraph develops around one controlling idea. Be careful not to add new information in a concluding sentence.

Read the following paragraph. Discuss why the writer should write a new concluding sentence.

A Very Good Man

My father was a very good man. He wasn't rich or famous. He showed me how important it is to be a good person. Honesty and sincerity were the most important values he taught us. He always said, "Always tell the truth and you will always be happy with yourself." My father died when I was sixteen, but I still remember his advice. My mother was wonderful, too.

 Exercise 8. Writing assignment: my family

Step 1. Reread the sentences you wrote for Exercise 2 on page 49. Choose one of these questions to focus on.

Which of your relatives has influenced you the most? How? *or*

Which of your relatives is the most important in your life? Why?

Brainstorm and make notes about that person.

Step 2. Organize your notes using one of the methods from Unit One (chart, map, list).

Step 3. Write a title and a topic sentence.

_____

_____

_____

Step 4. Write the first draft of your paragraph.

_____

_____

_____

_____

_____

_____

_____

_____

_____

_____

_____

_____

_____

_____

_____

_____

_____

_____

_____

_____

Exercise 9. Revising assignment

Step 1. Exchange your paragraph with a partner. Read each other's stories.

Step 2. Is your partner's topic sentence clear? Are all of the sentences related to the topic? If not, tell your partner.

Step 3. Write two or three questions to your partner about his or her relative. Give your partner the questions. Answer the questions your partner gives you.

1. _____

_____

2. _____

_____

3. _____

_____

Step 4. Talk with your partner about this new information. Should you add it to your paragraph? Where does it fit best?

Step 5. Rewrite your paragraph, using some or all of the new information.

_____

_____

_____

_____

_____

_____

_____

_____

_____

_____

_____

_____

_____

_____

_____

_____

_____

D Journal Assignment

Here are some journal topics for the theme of this unit. Write about them in your journal. Write about one topic at a time.

- Ways I am different from my family
- Ways I am like my family
- Bad habits of a relative I love
- What the youngest member of my family is thinking about
- What I have never said to my mother (my father)
- A traditional family holiday meal—who prepares what? who cleans up?
- How my family would have lived in a different time or place
- Why my parents are (were) so happy
- Why my parents aren't (weren't) so happy
- What the day will be like when I see my family again

Education

A   Prewriting

1.

Ojai, California, population 8,000

2.

Shallow Water, Kansas, population 100

3.

New York, New York, population 7,500,000

Exercise 1. Building an argument   Look at the three schools in the pictures. Decide which school you would send a child to. List your reasons in the blanks provided.

> **EXAMPLES:** It is safe in the country.
>
> There are more cultural opportunities in a big city.

In the future, I would send a child to _____

My reasons:

1. _____

2. _____

3. _____

4. _____

5. _____

Now, find other students who have made the same choice as you have. Form a group. Compare your lists of reasons.

    Finally, write the reasons listed by each group on the board. Individuals from each group should be prepared to explain their reasons.

Exercise 2. Group writing using transitions   Work in the same group as in Exercise 1 to write a paragraph explaining the reasons for your decision. To write your paragraph, first reread everyone's reasons and decide which five ideas are the most important. Put the ideas in order. Some writers put the most important reason first, and others put it last. Don't forget to think of an interesting title and a strong topic sentence to show the focus of your paragraph.

    Use some of the following words to organize your writing.

First,	Fourth,
First of all,	Another reason is that . . .
Second,	In conclusion,
Next,	Finally,
Third,	

Write in the following blanks on page 60.

_____

_____

_____

_____

_____

_____

_____

_____

_____

_____

_____

_____

_____

_____

_____

_____

_____

Questions and Comments:

Exercise 3. Peer editing Exchange your paragraph with another group. Read the new paragraph and discuss it in your group. If you have questions for the writers of the paragraph, write the questions after the paragraph. Also, write one comment telling what you like most about the paragraph.

> **EXAMPLES:** *Your ideas are very interesting. We especially like the last one because we didn't think of it.*
>
> *Your title was great. It made us want to read more.*

Finally, read the questions and comments on your group paragraph and discuss them in your group.

 Exercise 4. Campus vocabulary Think about your school campus. If your school does not have a campus, think of a college or university you know well. Then answer these questions in complete sentences. Be sure to see Appendix XI on page 170 for additional academic vocabulary.

> **EXAMPLE:** Where do students register for classes?
>
> *They register for classes in the admissions office on the first floor of this building.*

1. Where do students find counseling help?

   _____

2. Where can students eat on campus?

   _____

3. Where is the English language office located?

   _____

4. Where can students use computers?

   _____

5. Where can students get help choosing classes?

   _____

6. Where can students apply for financial aid?

   _____

7. Where do students go if they feel sick?

_____

8. Where do students find out about careers and part-time employment?

_____

9. Where can students check out books?

_____

10. Where can students relax and talk together?

_____

Exercise 5. Quickwrite on educational goals   In five minutes, write as much as you can on the topic "My Educational Goals." Do not use a dictionary. Do not erase or worry about the form of your writing. Just write as rapidly and as much as you can.

_____

_____

_____

_____

_____

_____

_____

_____

_____

_____

_____

_____

_____

_____

_____

_____

_____

_____

_____

_____

Exchange your writing with a partner. Discuss the differences and similarities in your goals.

B Structure

Sentence Combining Chart

Relationship	Two independent clauses	Dependent and independent clause
Addition	**, and** I can sing well, **and** I can play the guitar like a professional.	
Cause and effect	**, so** It rained, **so** the picnic was cancelled.	**because** **Because** it rained, the picnic was cancelled. The picnic was cancelled **because** it rained.
Contrast	**, but** I tried, **but** I couldn't understand.	**although (even though/though)** **Although** I tried, I couldn't understand. I couldn't understand **even though** I tried.
Choice	**, or** You can do it now, **or** I will do it later.	
Time		**before/after/ as soon as/since/ when/while/ whenever** **When** he arrived, I left. I have been here **since** the room opened.

Exercise 1. Joining sentences with time subordinators   Combine the sentences using one of the subordinators of time. See the chart on page 64. There may be more than one way to combine each pair of sentences.

> **EXAMPLE:** I was daydreaming. The teacher was explaining the assignment.
>
> I was daydreaming while the teacher was explaining the assignment.

Subordinators

The following connecting words and phrases are used to join two sentences when there is a relationship of time between them. They are called subordinators. Here are some subordinators.

after   as soon as   before   since   when   whenever   while

A subordinator introduces a *dependent clause*. Like an *independent clause*, a *dependent clause* has a subject and a verb, but it *depends* on an *independent clause* to complete its meaning. A dependent clause cannot be a sentence.

> **EXAMPLES:** We used to play baseball **after school was over.**
>
> Juan did his homework **as soon as he got home.**
>
> I have been studying English **since I was in seventh grade.***
>
> Ana used to chew gum **whenever we had a test.**
>
> Grigori was listening to the radio **while he was studying for the test.**
>
> *Use a perfect tense in the independent clause when you use **since.**

You need to use a comma to separate the *dependent clause* from the *independent clause* when the *dependent clause* comes first in the sentence.

> **EXAMPLES:** **After** school was over, we used to play baseball.
>
> **As soon as** he got home, Juan did his homework.*
>
> *In these sentences the subject in both clauses is the same person. Usually, you mention the subject's name in the first clause and then use a pronoun in the second clause.

> **EXAMPLES:** As soon as **Juan** got home, **he** did his homework.
>
> While **Grigori** was studying for the test, **he** was listening to the radio.

---

1. Jose listened to the radio. He was studying English.

   _____

2. Eduardo got home from work at 6 P.M. He studied English.

   _____

3. Kazu was 22 years old. He was accepted at Northwestern College.

   _____

4. Karl has been studying computers. He came here.

   _____

5. Svetlana studied a lot. She took the test.

   _____

6. Yuri started an adult education class. He arrived in this city.

   _____

7. Maria calls her sister. She has problems in class.

   _____

8. Max had never used a computer. He took a writing class.

   _____

9. Miwako bought a sweatshirt. She was looking for her class text in
   the bookstore.

   _____

10. Kang Sun returned to Korea. She saved enough money for a ticket.

    _____

11. Rosalina has not been lonely in class. She started making friends.

    _____

12. Roberto has been teaching in the ESL Department. He got his master's degree.

    _____

Writing to Learn: *From Paragraph to Essay*

Exercise 2. Using time subordinators   Think about your classmates and your teacher. Write ten sentences about them using time subordinators.

EXAMPLES: When the teacher called on Aurelio, he was reading a magazine.

Lin had never talked to me before we worked together in a group.

1. _____

2. _____

3. _____

4. _____

5. _____

6. _____

7. _____

8. _____

9. _____

10. _____

More Subordinating Conjunctions

There are other words that function the same way as the time words that you just practiced. Some of the most common subordinating conjunctions are **because** to show cause and effect and **though, although,** and **even though** to show contrast. They, too, combine independent clauses and dependent clauses.

EXAMPLES: I was often late for school. I had to help my mother.

I was often late for school **because I had to help my mother.**

I did my best. I was very nervous.

I did my best **even though I was very nervous.**

I did my best **although I was very nervous.**

Use a comma when the clause begins the sentence.

EXAMPLE: **Because** I had to help my mother, I was often late for school.

Exercise 3. More subordinating conjunctions Combine the following sentences using **because, though, although,** or **even though.** Then rewrite each sentence with the dependent clause at the beginning. (Be sure to use the noun first and the pronoun second.)

EXAMPLE: Keiko cannot work off-campus. She has a student visa.

Keiko cannot work off-campus because she has a student visa.
Because Keiko has a student visa, she cannot work off-campus.

1. I registered for only one class this semester. I have to work at night.

_____

_____

2. My sister can take only four units this semester. She cannot afford more tuition.

_____

_____

3. Pedro passed the course. He failed the final exam.

_____

_____

4. Philippe cannot apply for financial assistance. He isn't a resident student.

_____

_____

5. Takahiro did not get a scholarship. He had a high GPA.

_____

_____

6. Mai got a "C" on her paper. She rewrote it several times.

_____

_____

Exercise 4. Identifying dependent and independent clauses Read each of the following sentences carefully. Underline the dependent clause once. Underline the independent clause twice.

 EXAMPLE: <u>Because I work during the day,</u> <u><u>I have to study English at night.</u></u>

1. I like to do homework while I listen to the radio.

2. When I watch a video in the language lab, I usually take notes.

3. As soon as he arrived in class, he put his homework on the desk.

4. I couldn't do my homework before I came to class.

5. She answered my questions whenever I asked her.

6. I have used up three notebooks since the start of this semester.

7. Whenever I have a little free time, I try to study vocabulary.

8. Since Ali got off the plane, he has been speaking English.

9. After I attended a few classes, I really began to understand my new instructor.

10. You should not give up when a course is difficult.

Exercise 5. Completing incomplete sentences Each of the following sentences is incomplete because it contains only a dependent clause. Remember, a dependent clause needs an independent clause to form a sentence. Complete each sentence with your own independent clause.

 EXAMPLE: After I write my first draft, <u>I read it and make changes.</u>

1. After I finish a difficult exam _____

2. Before I began to study here _____

3. When I finish ESL classes _____

4. Since I enrolled in this class _____

5. Whenever I use a computer _____

6. _____ while I'm a student at this college.

7. _____ as soon as I get my degree.

8. _____ because I didn't do the homework last night.

9. _____ after I become fluent in English.

10. _____ since my first English class.

Exercise 6. Editing for sentence fragments of time A sentence fragment is an incomplete sentence. Each of the items in Exercise 5 is a sentence fragment. You have practiced creating whole sentences by adding an independent clause to the fragments. Now read this story. Correct the sentence fragments. Combine sentences where possible. (There is more than one way to combine sentences in this paragraph.) Rewrite on the next page.

Ray Wong, A Busy Teacher

Ray Wong starts his day. When he leaves his home at six o'clock every morning. He commutes to work. It takes a half hour. He teaches English at Cody High School, thirty miles away. Whenever he arrives in town early. Eats breakfast at the Sunflower Café. After breakfast, Ray drives to Cody High. He gets there ten minutes. Before first period. His first period class is freshman English. Second period is another section of freshman English. After those classes finish. Ray has senior honors English. Ray advises the poetry club. He eats lunch during the fourth period. When lunch is over. Ray rushes off-campus to teach a special English class in the center of town. It's back to campus for sixth period junior English. Seventh period Ray has a planning period. He plans his lessons and corrects papers. During eighth period. When he sometimes works with ESL students one on one. The school bell rings. Ray's day is not over. He stays after school to work with students on the school newspaper. Most school days, Ray doesn't get home until six-thirty. He's always late for dinner.

Ray Wong, A Busy Teacher

_____

_____

_____

_____

_____

_____

_____

_____

_____

_____

_____

_____

_____

_____

_____

_____

_____

_____

_____

_____

C **Writing and Editing**

Exercise 1. Writing assignment: my best teacher

Step 1. Think about the best teacher you have ever had. What grade were you in? What was the teacher's name? What did he or she teach? Why did you like this teacher?

Draw a picture of that teacher in the space provided. Then write down the reasons that you liked this teacher. Write an adjective that describes those reasons. Write a detail that gives an example of the adjective.

My Best Teacher

_____
(name)

_____
(grade/subject)

a. _____
(adjective)

_____

_____
(example or explanation)

b. _____
(adjective)

_____

_____
(example or explanation)

c. _____
(adjective)

_____

_____
(example or explanation)

Writing to Learn: *From Paragraph to Essay*

Step 2. Show your drawings to your classmates. Talk about your teacher. Answer the questions in Step 1. Read each reason, adjective, and detail.

Step 3. Use your notes from page 72 to write a paragraph about your best teacher. Include a strong topic sentence and examples to support it. Do not forget to include an interesting title. Remember to stay focused on your topic.

Exercise 2. Writing assignment: my worst teacher

Step 1. Think about the worst teacher you have ever had. What grade were you in? What was the teacher's name? What did he or she teach? Why did you dislike this teacher? Draw a picture of that teacher in the space provided. Then write down the reasons that you disliked this teacher. Write an adjective that describes those reasons. Write a detail that gives an example of the adjective.

My Worst Teacher

_____
(name)

_____
(grade/subject)

a. _____
(adjective)

_____

_____
(example or explanation)

b. _____
(adjective)

_____

_____
(example or explanation)

c. _____
(adjective)

_____

_____
(example or explanation)

Step 2. Show your drawings to your classmates. Talk about your teacher. Answer the questions in Step 1. Read each reason, adjective, and detail.

Writing to Learn: *From Paragraph to Essay*

Step 3. Use your notes from page 74 to write a paragraph about your worst teacher. Include a strong topic sentence and examples to support it. Do not forget to include an interesting title. Remember to stay focused on your topic.

_____

_____

_____

_____

_____

_____

_____

_____

_____

_____

_____

_____

_____

_____

_____

_____

Unit 3: Education

75

Exercise 3. Vocabulary expansion Look at these adjectives. Write them in the categories below. Would you use these words to describe a good teacher, a bad teacher, or are they not relevant? After you complete the exercise, you may want to revise your writing by adding or changing adjectives.

funny grouchy organized knowledgeable
beautiful disorganized
hypocritical strict cute encouraging
abusive intelligent disrespectful hardworking
warm respectful fair unfair inspiring
enthusiastic boring polite rude

A Good Teacher	A Bad Teacher	Not Relevant

Writing to Learn: From Paragraph to Essay

Exercise 4. Revising your writing   Choose one of your paragraphs to revise. Choose either your best or your worst teacher. Reread the paragraph you chose. Then answer these questions about it.

1. Is the topic sentence clear and interesting?

   ☐ Yes

   ☐ No

   ☐ It could be better.

2. Do you give more than one reason why you chose this teacher to write about?

   ☐ Yes

   ☐ I could add more.

3. Do you have an adjective and a detailed example for each reason?

   ☐ Yes

   ☐ I need to add adjectives and detailed examples.

4. Are all the sentences related to your main idea?

   ☐ Yes

   ☐ I need to cut one or two.

5. Do you have a good concluding sentence?

   ☐ Yes

   ☐ Not yet

6. Did you think of an interesting title?

   ☐ Yes

   ☐ I need to think of one.

If all of your answers are *yes*, you can submit your paper to your instructor. If not, make the changes you need to make. Then submit the paper.

Exercise 5. Practice editing a paragraph like yours Sometimes it helps to look at the work of other writers to improve your own. Look at the process of writing a paragraph like yours. A student, Jose Miranda, wrote a paragraph about his favorite teacher.

Here are his notes.

Notes:

Mrs. Gabriela Castro

psychology

reason #1: intelligent, she has a good opinion about life

reason #2: exciting, she made the classes very interesting and exciting

reason #3: sophisticated, she loves to travel often and to talk with people from different cultures

Interesting and Exciting Teacher

Read his first draft.

Mrs. Gabriela Castro was an intelligent and exciting teacher she always made the class very interesting and exciting because she showed many examples and asked many questions about her experience. She had a good opinion about life because she traveled often. She had three children of her own. She talked about all the places that she visited and the people's life styles. She taught me psychology. I remember her very well, she was a good influence in my life.

Look at Jose's first draft again while you read and answer these questions.

1. Is there a focus? _____

   If there is, what is it? What does the writer want to show about Mrs. Castro?

   _____

2. Are there details to support or explain the main idea? _____

   Underline each detail or example two times.

3. Is there any information that does not support the focus? _____

   Cross out unnecessary information.

4. Is there a concluding sentence? _____

   Underline the concluding sentence three times.

5. Is there a title? _____

Now look at Jose's second draft and answer the preceding questions again.

Thanks, Mrs. Castro

Mrs. Gabriela Castro was an intelligent and exciting teacher. She taught me psychology. She was interesting and exciting because she always showed many examples and asked many questions in the class. She liked to travel a lot and talk to people; therefore, she was sophisticated. I liked to ask questions about her experiences because she had a good attitude about life. I remember her very well. Thank you very much, Mrs. Gabriela Castro.

D   Journal Assignment

Here are some topics for the theme of this unit. There are three ways to write in the journal: (1) write about any topic listed under **Write,** (2) draw and label any topic listed under **Draw,** and (3) read and write about any poem, article, story, or text given to you by your teacher under **Read and Respond.**

Write

Something I want to learn

How I learn best

A letter to my teacher

How schools in my country are

The five most important things I've learned

Draw

My elementary school classroom

The ideal classroom

A twenty-second century school

My graduation

What's in a student's backpack?

Read and Respond to a poem, article, story, or other text that your teacher gives to you.

A Journal Alternative   Write about the theme of education in any way you want to. You can think of your own topics.

Employment Application—The following is the continuation of an employment application that you began in Unit One. See Appendix XII on pages 171–173 for a complete application.

Education

School most recently attended:

Name _____ Location _____

Graduated?   ☐ Yes   ☐ No

If no, last grade completed _____

Now enrolled?   ☐ Yes   ☐ No

Sports or Activities _____

_____

_____

_____

_____

Work

A Prewriting

Exercise 1. Discussing the pictures Look at the pictures. Decide what each person is doing and what job each probably has. One person can complete the chart for pictures 1, 3, 5, and 7. The other person completes the chart for pictures 2, 4, 6, and 8. Tell each other your ideas. The listener can take notes in the chart. Do you agree with each other? Do you have other ideas?

	What job does this person have?	What is is s/he doing?	How much training did s/he need?	One good point about this job	One bad point about this job
Picture 1					
Picture 2					
Picture 3					
Picture 4					
Picture 5					
Picture 6					
Picture 7					
Picture 8					

Exercise 2. Discussing your job Think about the job you do or one you did in the past. If you have never worked, think about a job you are familiar with. Use the chart that follows to brainstorm the good and bad things about this job. Then talk to your partner about it.

Job: _____

Good things about this job	Bad things about this job
EXAMPLE: *good pay*	**EXAMPLE:** *long hours*

Exercise 3. Brainstorming job vocabulary How many job titles do you know? Try to fill in the chart below by writing at least one job next to each letter of the alphabet.

EXAMPLE: **A** _architect_____

A	_____	**N**	_____
B	_____	**O**	_____
C	_____	**P**	_____
D	_____	**Q**	_____
E	_____	**R**	_____
F	_____	**S**	_____
G	_____	**T**	_____
H	_____	**U**	_____
I	_____	**V**	_____
J	_____	**W**	_____
K	_____	**X**	_____
L	_____	**Y**	_____
M	_____	**Z**	_____

Exercise 4. Job interview vocabulary Read these adjectives and adjective phrases. Which ones best describe you to a potential employer? Check each word that describes you and write one reason why it does on page 86.

EXAMPLE: __X__ dependable

I always complete my work.

_____ calm under pressure

_____ creative

_____ dependable

_____ efficient

_____ friendly

_____ good with numbers

_____ other

_____ good with details

_____ hardworking

_____ organized

_____ prompt

_____ responsible

_____ skilled

Write your reasons in the blanks provided.

_____

_____

_____

_____

_____

_____

_____

_____

_____

_____

Exercise 5. Preparing for a job interview   Prepare yourself for an interview. Write down two or three of your strengths and one weakness. Be sure to give examples and explanations.

Interviews

During an interview, the interviewer may ask you to describe your strengths and weaknesses. This is difficult to do, especially when you must list your weaknesses.

   You have to say *something*, but you don't want to sound like a person who will become a bad employee. You can say something like, "People say I am a workaholic." The company may love to have such a hard worker! Another possible response is, "My coworkers and friends say I am too serious about my work because I always talk about it when I am away from the job. I always try to think of ways to do my job better."

   Of course, you should always tell the truth about yourself, but this is not the time to be shy or modest.

---

1. Strength _____

    Example _____

2. Strength _____

    Example _____

3. Strength _____

    Example _____

4. Strength _____

    Example _____

Exercise 6. Freewriting on your future career   Your topic is "My Future Career Plans." For five minutes, write as much as you can. In English, write everything that comes to mind. Do not worry about mistakes. Don't edit.

My Future Career Plans

_____

_____

_____

_____

_____

_____

_____

_____

_____

_____

_____

_____

_____

_____

_____

_____

_____

_____

_____

_____

_____

_____

_____

_____

_____

_____

_____

_____

_____

_____

 Exchange papers with your group mates. Keep exchanging until everyone in the group has read everyone else's paper. After reading, complete the following chart and talk about the similarities and differences in your plans. Talk about how you will accomplish your career goals.

Writing to Learn: *From Paragraph to Essay*

Similarities in our plans	Differences in our plans

B Structure

Sentence Combining Chart

Relationship	Two independent clauses	Independent clause and dependent clause	Two independent clauses
Addition	**, and** I can sing well, **and** I can play the guitar well.		
Cause and effect	**, so** It rained hard, **so** the picnic was cancelled.	**because** The picnic was cancelled **because** it rained hard.	**; therefore,** It rained hard; **therefore,** the picnic was cancelled.
Contrast	**, but** I tried very hard, **but** I couldn't understand her.	**although/even though/though** I couldn't understand her **although** I tried very hard.	**; however,** I tried very hard; **however,** I couldn't understand her.
Choice	**, or** You can do your homework now, **or** you can do it later.		
Time		**after/before/as soon as/since/when whenever/while** I have been here **since** six o'clock this morning.	

Writing to Learn: *From Paragraph to Essay*

Exercise 1. Connecting sentences with the transition words _therefore_ and _however_ Combine the pairs of sentences into one sentence using **therefore** or **however.**

> **EXAMPLE:** I need a job that doesn't require lifting heavy objects. I can't work for a moving company.
>
> _I need a job that doesn't require lifting heavy objects; therefore, I can't work for a moving company._

Transition words

The transition words **therefore** and **however** are used to join two sentences when there is a relationship between them of result or reason (_therefore_), or contrast (_however_). They are used in writing that has a formal style, such as an academic essay, a textbook passage, a newspaper or magazine article, a business letter, or a government document. Their everyday equivalents are _so_ for _therefore_ and _but_ for _however_.

Some other words that can be used as transitions are _thus, as a result, consequently,_ and _hence_ for _therefore,_ and _nevertheless_ for _however_.

When transition words join sentences, they usually occur between two sentences and are preceded by a semicolon (;) and followed by a comma (,). The sentences that they join are usually two independent clauses.

> **EXAMPLES:** Un Taek's work involves a lot of traveling; **therefore,** it keeps him out of town about half the year.
>
> Maria's job doesn't pay well; **however,** it allows her creative freedom.

The example sentences can be written as two separate sentences with the transition word beginning the second sentence. In that case, the transition word is followed by a comma.

> **EXAMPLES:** Un Taek's work involves a lot of traveling. **Therefore,** it keeps him out of town about half the year.
>
> Maria's job doesn't pay well. **However,** it allows her creative freedom.

---

1. Serafin wants to be a civil engineer. He is looking for an internship with a engineering company for the summer.

   _____

   _____

2. Vung would like to go back to school to study business. He doesn't have enough money to pay for his tuition.

_____

_____

3. No one likes to clean out bathrooms. Some janitors have to do it.

_____

_____

4. Business people can make quite a lot of money. Many of them have to work long hours for it.

_____

_____

5. Claudine is a cashier. She wants to be an artist.

_____

_____

6. Chizuko wants to travel. She would like to be a flight attendant.

_____

_____

7. Tomas had no idea how to serve dinner. He had a lot of problems his first day as a waiter.

_____

_____

8. Susana often feels upset. She never lets her customers know it.

_____

_____

Writing to Learn: *From Paragraph to Essay*

Exercise 2. Rewriting sentences with *therefore* and *however* When you write, you want to vary the structure of your sentences to make your writing more interesting. Rewrite the following sentences using **therefore** and **however.**

EXAMPLE: Sergio works fast, so he is an excellent busboy.
Sergio works fast; therefore, he is an excellent busboy.
Because Sergio works fast, he is an excellent busboy.
Although Sergio is an excellent cook, he is still a busboy.

1. Sergio knows how to set and clear tables, but he doesn't know how to take orders.

   _____

   _____

2. Maria is a receptionist, so speaking and listening skills are important for her.

   _____

   _____

3. Mario is from Mexico, but he works in a Japanese restaurant.

   _____

   _____

4. Although Young Joo is an excellent photographer, she works as a cashier.

   _____

   _____

5. Because Jin wants to work with technology, he is taking computer courses.

   _____

   _____

6. Mariana got a job for a pizza delivery company because she understands English very well.

   _____

   _____

7. Roberto always has a smile on his face, so his customers like him.

_____

_____

8. Emiko speaks English well, so she should be able to get a good job when she goes back to her country.

_____

_____

Exercise 3. Writing sentences with *therefore* and *however*   Complete the following sentences about yourself. Circle what is true for *you* in the first part of the sentences. Then complete the sentence.

> **EXAMPLE:** I am good with numbers /(I am not good with numbers;)therefore, I
> *never want to work in a bank.*

1. I am good with details / I am not good with details _____

_____

2. I am calm under pressure / I get nervous under pressure _____

_____

3. I am hardworking / I am easy-going _____

_____

4. I am dependable / I am happy-go-lucky* _____

_____

5. I am friendly / I am shy** _____

_____

*not worried about the future, focused on the pleasure of the moment
**uncomfortable in front of other people, usually quiet

Writing to Learn: From Paragraph to Essay

6. I am skilled in word processing / I am not skilled in word processing _____

_____

7. I am well-organized / I am disorganized _____

_____

8. I am prompt / I am always late _____

_____

9. I am efficient / I like to take my time _____

_____

10. I am creative / I am good at following directions _____

_____

Run-on Sentences

Run-on sentences are two or more sentences (independent clauses) written together without proper connecting words or punctuation.

This is a run-on sentence: *I like my job my manager is very fair.*

One way to correct this run-on sentence is to add punctuation to separate the independent clauses.

EXAMPLE: *I like my job. My manager is very fair.*

Another way to correct this run-on sentence is by adding connecting words such as coordinating conjunctions, subordinators, or transitions.

EXAMPLE: *I like my job because my manager is very fair.*

In this example, it is better to add a connecting word because it helps to clarify meaning.

Exercise 4. Recognizing run-on sentences   Read the sentences that follow. Write **RO** next to run-on sentences. Write **CS** next to complete sentences. Rewrite the run-on sentences correctly.

_____   1.   Lila works long hours she gets very tired.

_____

_____   2.   My uncle manages a successful photocopy business.

_____

_____   3.   I like to work with numbers I plan to work in a bank some day.

_____

_____   4.   My job is hard it is boring, too.

_____

_____   5.   Sam clears the tables, puts on a new tablecloth, then he sets the table.

_____

_____   6.   Babysitters have a lot of responsibility, but they receive little pay.

_____

_____   7.   Tania knows how to use a computer for word processing now she wants to learn how to use a spreadsheet.

_____

_____   8.   Men often earn more than women for doing the same jobs.

_____

_____   9.   I interviewed for a job on Monday I didn't come to class.

_____

_____   10.   It is just my first day on the job I am making a lot of mistakes.

_____

Writing to Learn: _From Paragraph to Essay_

Exercise 5. A story: "Moving Up the Ladder" Read the story about Kim Tae Sam. In the blank spaces, write words that help to tell the story. Some of the words you might want to use are **and, but, so, or, however, because, therefore, when, after, before,** and **although.**

Moving Up the Ladder

Kim Tae Sam was born in a farming village in Chollado, South Korea. _____ he was small, he used to help his parents plant rice in the field. He was a good student, _____ his parents sent him to school in Kwangju, a large city. He would visit his parents' village on school vacations. The rest of the year he remained in the city to study. Tae Sam studied hard _____ did well on the entrance examination for university. He attended a university in Seoul, far from his family. He only visited them in summer. During winter break, he studied English at a language school in Seoul.

Tae Sam chose to study computer science. He knew that there were many opportunities in this field _____ it was a new field. Tae Sam graduated from the university. His parents made the trip to Seoul to attend the graduation. They felt uncomfortable. _____ the graduation ceremony, they went straight home. Tae Sam stayed in Seoul to look for a job. He got a job with an American company _____ he could speak English and he knew computers well.

_____ he had worked for two years in Seoul, the company sent him to New York to work in its headquarters there. Tae Sam was happy to have the chance to travel, _____ he was sad

_____ he would be very far away from home. In New York, Tae

Sam met a Korean-American woman, Oh Hae Ja. They fell in love. Hae Ja

was a teacher, _____ her work was very important to her. Tae Sam

loved her. _____ she was not really like women in Korea, _____

she did not speak Korean well.

Tae Sam's company was not doing well. His boss told him he had to

return to Korea within six months. He asked Hae Ja to go back with him.

She would not go. _____, Tae Sam quit the company.

_____ he quit, he had to tell his parents that he would not return

to Korea. They were very upset. Then Tae Sam used his savings to buy a

small convenience store. _____ he did that, he and Hae Ja made

plans to marry. Tae Sam worked seven days a week, twenty hours a day

in the store. One day Tae Sam realized that his life had changed. He was

always tired. _____ he could not think of anything but his store.

What had happened to his career?

C Writing and Editing

Exercise 1. Informal letter writing Imagine that you are Tae Sam. You are going to write a letter to your American friend, Arthur, who lives and works in Korea to explain why you have decided to stay in the United States. Write that letter in the blanks provided.

Writing to Learn: *From Paragraph to Essay*

New York, New York

August 1, 2000

Dear Arthur,

_____

_____

_____

_____

_____

_____

_____

_____

_____

_____

_____

_____

_____

_____

_____

Your friend,

Tae Sam

Exercise 2. Interview research   In Exercise 6 on pages 87–89, you wrote about your career plans. Like most students, you probably have questions about how you can reach your goals. There are many places to get answers to questions about careers, employment, training, and education. Write down two ideas of your own about where you can find out information on these topics. Then share your ideas with your group.

My ideas

1. _____

2. _____

Others' ideas

1. _____

2. _____

3. _____

4. _____

5. _____

Write some questions that you would like to ask about reaching your career goals. Choose the best place from the preceding list. Then go and find some answers.

EXAMPLE: Do I need a degree to teach in preschool?

_____

_____

_____

_____

_____

_____

_____

_____

_____

_____

_____

Exercise 3. Writing a summary of the information you found   Organize the information you found into a paragraph that summarizes the important things someone should know about your career field. Find other people in the class who have chosen a similar or the same career field. Exchange information.

Career: _____

_____

_____

_____

_____

_____

_____

_____

_____

_____

_____

_____

_____

_____

_____

_____

Exercise 4. Job search—an interactive group writing assignment

Step 1. Form a company. Decide what kind of company you will have. Invent a name. Choose a president or Chief Executive Officer (CEO), vice president, administrative assistant, and a director of human resources. Decide on a job that your company needs to fill.

Step 2. Use the outline on pages 104–105 as a guide. Write down the job title. Brainstorm about the qualifications you want applicants to have. Brainstorm about the job responsibilities. How much is the salary? What are the benefits?

Step 3. Look at some job advertisements in a newspaper and the sample on page 106. Notice the kind of information that is given in job ads. Write a job announcement for the job that is available in your company. It will be more interesting if you add your company logo or a picture to the announcement. Make sure that the announcement is clear and correct. Make sure it has all the important information.

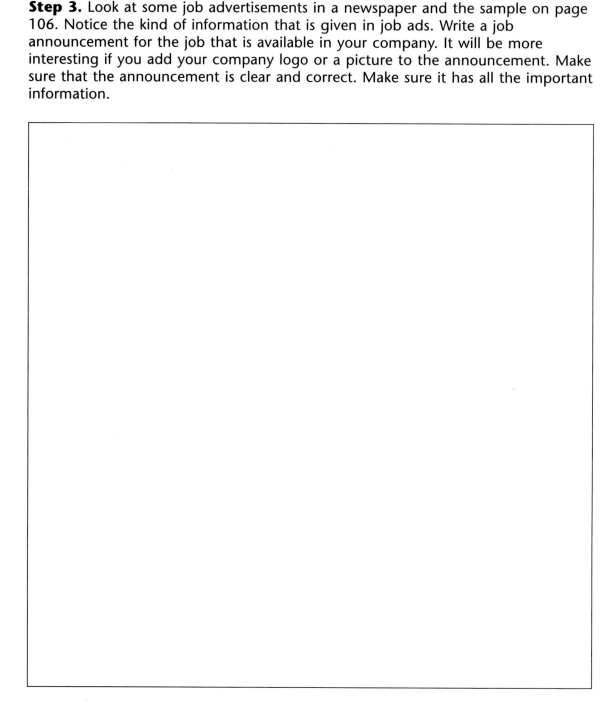

Step 4. Copy your job announcement and post the job announcement in the classroom.

Step 5. Now imagine that you are someone looking for a job. Choose one of the jobs posted in your classroom. Write a letter of application.* You can follow the sample letter on page 107.

*You should work with a classmate to revise your letter before you send it to the company.

Writing to Learn: *From Paragraph to Essay*

Step 6. Go back to your company and read your mail from job applicants. Underline all the sentences in each letter that show the applicant's qualifications for the job. Choose two or three applicants to interview. Announce your choices.

Step 7. Look at the sample interview questions below and on page 105. Use the space provided to write eight interview questions for your job vacancy. Decide who in your company will interview the applicants and answer their questions.

Step 8. Interview the applicants. You can do this in groups, or the whole class can observe each group interview. Then, have a short company meeting to decide whom to hire. Announce whom you have hired and why.

Company Outline

Company name _____

President or CEO _____

Vice President _____

Director of Human Resources _____

Administrative Assistant _____

We need to hire a (job title) _____

Job responsibilities: _____

Skills/education required: _____

Salary or hourly wage: _____

Benefits: _____

Sample Interview Questions

What are your strong points (strengths)?

What are your weak points (weaknesses)?

Why do you want this job?

Why do you want to work for this company?

How are you qualified for this position?

Are you currently employed?

What do you do now?

If you quit your last job, why did you quit?

Explain one problem you had that you solved successfully.

What would you do if you saw a fellow employee stealing from the company?

The following questions cannot be asked during a job interview in the United States:

What is your religion?

Have you ever been arrested?

Are you married?

Do you have children?

Do you plan to have children?

Company Interview Questions

1. _____

2. _____

3. _____

4. _____

5. _____

6. _____

7. _____

8. _____

Decide who will interview the candidates. Will it be one person or will you take turns?

Exercise 5. Revising your job letter After writing your letter of application for the job, exchange letters with a classmate and answer these questions.

1. Are there three paragraphs?	☐ yes	☐ no
2. Does the first paragraph clearly explain the purpose of the letter?	☐ yes	☐ no
3. Does the second paragraph explain the writer's qualifications for the job?	☐ yes	☐ no
4. Does the last paragraph explain when the applicant is available for an interview and how to contact him or her?	☐ yes	☐ no
5. Is the form and punctuation of the letter similar to the sample letter?	☐ yes	☐ no
6. Is the letter neat?	☐ yes	☐ no
7. Is the spelling correct?	☐ yes	☐ no

If the answer to any of these questions is no, rewrite your letter after correcting and revising it. Use the sample letter on page 107 as a guide, but do not copy it.

Job Advertisement

Daily News
CLASSIFIED ADVERTISEMENTS

The Redmore Resort Hotel is looking for an energetic, creative individual with strong communication skills and extraordinary interpersonal skills to join our team. Experience coordinating weddings and conferences preferred, but will consider training a motivated, hardworking person.

   Job description   Events Coordinator (full-time, administrative)
   Salary: negotiable
   Benefits: full medical/dental coverage for employee and dependents
   Stock options
   Retirement package
   Two weeks paid vacation a year
   Six paid sick days a year

Forward resumé and letter of interest to Janet Jordan, Director of Personnel, The Redmore Resort Hotel, 1000 Coast View Road, Honolulu, HI 96877.

Job Application Letter

Read the letter below, written in response to the advertisement.

1551 Keeaumakaii Street
Honolulu, HI 96877
June 5, 2000

Janet Jordan
Director of Personnel
The Redmore Resort Hotel
1000 Coast View Road
Honolulu, HI 96877

Dear Ms. Jordan:

I would like to apply for the position of Special Events Coordinator that you advertised in the Sunday issue of the *Daily News.* I have long admired your world-famous resort, and I would like the opportunity to be part of your first-class team of hotel professionals.

You are looking for someone with energy, creativity, and extraordinary interpersonal skills. The letters of reference attached will show you that I am that person. They will also show that I have three years of experience in the hotel industry as a waitress and desk clerk. In addition, I have had one season of experience as a cruise recreation director. Moreover, I have recently completed a Hotel and Restaurant Culinary Program. As a result, I have learned a good deal about preparing food for large events.

I believe that I have the qualifications, energy, and enthusiasm that you are looking for in a Special Events Coordinator. I am available for an interview at your convenience. I look forward to meeting you. I can be reached at 503/966-5551. My email address is resortclaud@usol.com.

Sincerely,

Claudia Vasquez
Claudia Vasquez

D Journal Assignment

Write about one of the following topics. Then show your writing to someone who reads English but is not in your class. Get his or her reaction. What does he/she think of your ideas?

- My dream job
- The best job I ever had
- The worst job I ever had
- How I feel about my present job
- What's most important to me in a job?
- What makes a good boss?
- If I were running a company
- Are we paid fairly for the work we do?

Alternative journal assignment   Look through the newspaper classified advertisements. Pick out an advertisement for a job that you would like. In your journal, write why you are qualified for the job.

Here is a continuation of the Employment Application that you completed in Units One and Three. See Appendix XII on pages 171–173 for a complete sample application.

Work Experience

Three most recent jobs within the last five years

Company _____ Position _____

Dates worked: From _____ To _____

Salary _____ Supervisor _____

Reason for leaving _____

_____

Company _____ Position _____

Dates worked: From _____ To _____

Salary _____ Supervisor _____

Reason for leaving _____

_____

Company _____ Position _____

Dates worked: From _____ To _____

Salary _____ Supervisor _____

Reason for leaving _____

_____

Leisure and Recreation

A   Prewriting

Exercise 1. Vocabulary warm-up   Use the chart that follows to write down the activities you see happening in the picture on page 111. In the left-hand column of the chart, write *like* if you like doing the activity or *dislike* if you dislike doing the activity. Compare your list with the lists of the other people in your group.

Like or Dislike	Activity

Unit 5: Leisure and Recreation

Exercise 2. Talking about leisure activities   Take turns telling about the things you do in your free time. Use the chart on page 110 if it is helpful to you. If you do not understand the activity your group mate is talking about, ask that person to explain it to you.

Next, interview one person from another group about what he or she likes to do during his or her free time. Find out *when, how often, where,* and *with whom* your classmate does the activity. Write your questions in the space provided before you ask them to your classmate. Take notes as your partner answers your questions.

EXAMPLE: **What** _____

_____

_____

When _____

_____

_____

How often _____

_____

Where _____

_____

_____

With whom _____

_____

_____

Writing to Learn: *From Paragraph to Essay*

Exercise 3. Freewriting—vacation For ten minutes, write as much as you can on the topic "Vacation." Then read your writing to your group.

Vacation

_____

_____

_____

_____

_____

_____

_____

_____

_____

_____

_____

_____

_____

_____

_____

_____

_____

_____

_____

_____

_____

_____

Exercise 4. Sorting ideas   When people have free time, they do many different things. They exercise and do sports such as volleyball, soccer, and swimming. They relax with a book or in front of the TV. They work in the garden, do chores around the house, and work on their cars. They visit friends, go out to dinner, and go for hikes in the mountains. Some people even use their free time to help others by volunteering at hospitals, senior citizen centers, and homeless shelters.

Lou's activities in the list that follows are not sorted. That is, the activities are not put into similar groups. Rewrite the activities into groups that are similar in some way. For example, you might have a group of activities that requires a lot of energy and causes a person to get tired after doing any of them. You might have another group of activities that someone would do with friends. There are many different ways of sorting. The way you sort is up to you. You do *not* need to include all the activities.

Lou's list of free-time activities

play bass in an adult ed jazz combo

listen to my CDs

practice classical guitar

swim for an hour every other morning

play tennis occasionally

do gardening work and yard work on weekends

write some short stories when there is time

read *The New Yorker* every week

go for a bike ride with Marilynn

walk my dog, Lucy, every morning at six

rent a video once in a while

listen to the radio every morning

read about teaching

read novels, poetry, and short stories

go for breakfast with my friends at the Rose Café

go to a movie

attend a concert about once every two months

watch sports on TV every day

Give each category a title. List the activities on the following chart.

Exercise 5. Writing a first draft   Write a paragraph for each group of Lou's activities listed in Exercise 4. Remember to introduce the paragraph with a topic sentence that tells the reader what the main idea is in the paragraph. (See Unit One, pages 22–24, for a reminder about topic sentences.)

> **EXAMPLE:** Lou likes sports and plays them quite often.

Lou's Activities

_____

_____

_____

_____

_____

_____

_____

_____

_____

_____

_____

_____

_____

_____

_____

_____

_____

_____

_____

_____

_____

_____

_____

_____

_____

_____

_____

_____

_____

_____

_____

_____

_____

_____

_____

B Structure

Exercise 1. Writing transition sentences   Now that you have written several paragraphs about Lou's activities, read the paragraphs again. Answer these questions about them.

1. Do they seem to go well together, or do they need something to make them fit more closely together?

2. Does paragraph one lead the reader easily to paragraph two, or do you need a *transition sentence*?

Transition Sentences

A *transition sentence* moves the reader from one idea group (paragraph) to another idea group (paragraph) by making a connection between the ideas.

EXAMPLE: Lou likes sports a lot, but he also likes music.

Notice that a transition sentence usually gives you an idea of what the topic of the next paragraph will be. In the example above, the next topic is music. Another thing to notice is that writers often use the same sentence to change topics and to introduce a new topic, usually at the beginning of the new paragraph. This means that a transition sentence can also be a topic sentence for a paragraph.

Now read the paragraphs you wrote for Exercise 5 on pages 116–117. If you do not have transition sentences, add them. Underline your transition sentences. Then, exchange your paper with a partner.

1. Are your transition sentences similar or different? _____

2. Are the transition sentences clear and helpful to you as a reader? _____

Exercise 2. Using *such as, for example,* and *for instance* Complete the following sentences. Give two or three examples for each sentence.

EXAMPLE: There are many ways to spend a Friday night such as going dancing,
example one

going out to eat, or going to a movie.
example two   example three

Such as, for example, for instance

Giving examples when you write makes your writing more interesting and makes your point of view clearer.
 Such as, for example, and **for instance** are phrases that introduce examples. Notice the punctuation in the examples.

EXAMPLES: There are many warm weather sports **such as** swimming, beach volleyball, and water skiing.

There are many warm weather sports, **for example,** swimming, beach volleyball, and water skiing.

There are many warm weather sports, **for instance,** swimming, beach volleyball, and water skiing.

For example and **for instance** require commas. **Such as** does not require a comma.

1. There are many team sports such as _____

_____

2. I like all kinds of music, for example, _____

_____

3. My friend has been all over the world to many interesting places, for instance,

_____

_____

4. There are many places to stay on a vacation such as _____

_____

5. I like to do a lot of different things on my day off, for example, _____

_____

6. There are many things to do on a Sunday morning such as _____

_____

7. I love to watch soap operas, for instance, _____

_____

8. There are many popular card games such as _____

_____

Exercise 3. Creating sentences by grouping like things   Read through the following list with your partner. Group those things that go together in the chart. Then write a sentence about them.

EXAMPLE: **winter sports:** skiing, snowboarding, sleighing
I like all sorts of winter sports, for example, skiing, snowboarding, and sleighing.

Italian food	surfing	the Statue of Liberty	cookies
comedies	checkers	backgammon	chess
bridge	swimming	the Eiffel Tower	hearts
soccer	sailing	cake	baseball
Korean food	French food	adventure movies	the Sphinx
poker	candy	horror movies	football

Category	Example	Example	Example
winter sports	skiing	snowboarding	sleighing

1. _____

2. _____

3. _____

4. _____

5. _____

6. _____

7. _____

8. _____

Writing to Learn: *From Paragraph to Essay*

Exercise 4. Editing for fragments and run-on sentences   Read this paragraph. Then rewrite it, correcting the sentence fragments and run-on sentences.

Enjoying My Day Off

My day off work was just wonderful my brother lent me his car. I drove to the mall. Where I found lots of things in a stationery store that would make good presents for example diaries, calendars, and fountain pens the holidays are coming up so I was thinking about buying presents for my family. First, I went to look for a gift for my mother. She likes household gadgets. Such as can openers, recipe holders, and little reading lights. I found just the right thing. A perfect gift. It wasn't too expensive. I got hungry from so much shopping. So I ate a lot. For instance I had a big salty pretzel, a chocolate covered donut, and a slice of pizza with pineapple and bacon on it. My stomach hurt. When I got home. But I was happy because I had made a good start on my holiday shopping.

Enjoying My Day Off

_____

_____

_____

_____

_____

_____

_____

_____

_____

_____

_____

_____

_____

_____

_____

_____

_____

_____

 Exercise 5. Talking about your free-time activities First, use the following chart to categorize your free-time activities. Then, with your partner, discuss your free-time activities. Use **such as, for example,** and **for instance** in your conversation.

Outdoor (exercise)	Indoor (games and hobbies)	Music	Reading	TV, Video, Movies

Writing to Learn: *From Paragraph to Essay*

C Writing and Editing

Exercise 1. The form of an essay To understand the structure of an essay, it is helpful to analyze one. Read the following essay and do the exercise that follows it.

My Guitars

Most people have a hobby, something they like to do whenever they can. My hobby is the guitar. I am not the greatest musician in the world, but I have become good enough to entertain myself, my family, and my friends. I have also made a little money playing in clubs and for parties and weddings. I have been playing guitar for over thirty years now. In that time, I have owned several guitars. Each one was special to me, and each one brought a different kind of music to me.

I can remember my first guitar quite well. It was a cheap, Harmony, steel-string guitar that hurt my fingers when I played it for more than ten minutes. Despite the pain that Harmony gave me, it gave me a lot of pleasure, too. When I learned a new song on the guitar, I would rush out to my friends to play it for them. Then the Beatles came to the United States. After seeing the Beatles, I decided my scratchy-sounding Harmony was not good enough. I wanted an electric guitar. I wanted to be a Beatle. Of course, I still was not a very good guitar player, and I could hardly read music. Nevertheless, I begged my parents to buy me an electric guitar. One Saturday, my father took me to a music store and bought one for me.

Ah, my first electric guitar! It was a Gibson ES-355, sunburst with double cutaways. What an instrument! It had two volume controls, two tone controls, and a position switch that gave different sounds. That

Gibson changed my musical life because I had to promise my parents to take guitar lessons. I took lessons for about two years off and on. My teachers were jazz guitarists. That caused a problem for me. When it came time to form a rock band, which every young person with a guitar wanted to do after seeing the Beatles, I was given the honor of being the lead guitarist. At that time, in imitation of the Beatles, most rock groups were quartets consisting of drums, lead guitar, rhythm guitar, and bass guitar. That was me. However, there was a problem with that. I wanted to sound like George Harrison, the Beatles' lead guitarist, but I sounded like a jazz guitarist instead. Fortunately, I learned, little by little, to play rock 'n' roll. As I improved on the guitar, my musical tastes became broader. I became interested in learning to play classical guitar.

I bought my first classical guitar about ten years after I started learning to play guitar. My classical guitar was the work of an old Italian instrument maker in New York City. He put a lot of love into the instrument, and I learned to appreciate the music that guitar was meant to play such as the music of Bach, Vivaldi, and Villa-Lobos. From that time on, I began to teach myself how to play the classical guitar. To this day, I am still learning. I try to play my Segovia etudes often, and every Christmastime I work on my version of Bach's "Jesu, Joy of Man's Desiring."

In addition to my continuing study of classical guitar, I have come back to the jazz music that my guitar teachers tried to teach me years ago. When I played rock 'n' roll, I used to think that jazz was boring. Now it is a never-ending source of creative guitar playing for me. I guess if I had to label myself as a guitarist, I would call myself a jazz guitarist now. I have learned the songs of some great American jazz songwriters, for example, George Gershwin, Cole Porter, Duke Ellington, and Fats Waller. My guitar has been my passport to different musical worlds, and each world has offered me a different musical culture. Lately, I have become interested in Irish music and traditional North American folk music. My trusted companion on all these new musical journeys has been my guitar. It is always at hand. I do not travel for long periods of time without it. When I think of other hobbies, I can't help but feel I am very lucky to have started studying the guitar. It has been one of the joys of my life.

1. Write *introduction, body,* or *conclusion* next to each paragraph in the essay. How many paragraphs are there in this essay? _____

2. Underline the sentence in the introduction that tells the general subject of the essay. This is the topic.

3. Underline twice the sentence(s) in the introduction that give(s) the writer's idea(s) about the topic. This is called the thesis statement.

4. What do you think the purposes of the introduction are? What does the writer do in the first paragraph?

   _____

   _____

   _____

   _____

5. Circle any transition sentences in each paragraph, sentences that lead to another idea about the topic.

6. Put a star at the beginning of the topic sentence for each paragraph.

7. Put parentheses ( ) around each detail, supporting idea, or example in the paragraphs of the body.

8. Rewrite the sentence that you think is the most important one in the conclusion.

_____

_____

_____

9. What do you think is the main purpose of the conclusion? What does the writer want to do in the conclusion?

_____

_____

_____

10. What do you like about the essay? _____

_____

_____

 Exercise 2. Writing the introduction and the conclusion

Writing Introductions and Conclusions

For many writers, writing the *body* of an essay is easier than writing the introduction and conclusion. Why? Because the body of the essay is where all of your information is. Writing the introduction and the conclusion may require more creativity to make interesting paragraphs. At the same time, the introduction and the conclusion are very important because they are the first and last impressions that your reader will have of you as a writer.

The Introduction

Purpose:

1. Get the reader's attention
2. Introduce the topic (Recreation)
3. State the thesis
4. Orient the reader to your method of development

Techniques for getting the reader's attention:

1. Begin with a question

   "What do you do in your free time?"

2. Begin with a general statement

   "Everyone has a favorite leisure activity."

3. Begin with a surprising fact or statistic

   "A recent government survey states that people who relax every day for an hour live longer."

4. Begin with a famous quotation or proverb

   "All work and no play makes Jack a dull boy. The same is true for Jill."

5. Begin with a short personal story (an anecdote)

   "Last summer, while driving across the United States, I thought about how important it was to have a time in your life when nothing is planned."

6. Begin with a historical reference or refer to a current event

   "The ancient Japanese preferred to vacation in fall and spring. I feel the same way."

Dangers to avoid

Do not try to say everything in the introduction. Save your details and examples for the body of the essay. Do not write "My topic is . . ." or "I'm going to write about . . ."

For the following topic and thesis statement, use three different techniques to make an interesting introduction.

Topic: Movies

Thesis Statement: *Movies have created an international culture from which people around the world take their ideas of goodness, truth, and beauty.*

1. _____

   _____

2. _____

   _____

3. _____

   _____

The Conclusion

The conclusion is the last place for you to make your point. It is the last impression your reader has of you as a writer. Unfortunately, many writers run out of steam, and write very short, uninteresting conclusions to their essays.

Techniques

1. Summarize your main point
2. End with a question
3. End with a famous quotation that illustrates your main point
4. Ask for the reader to do something related to the topic

Dangers to avoid

1. Don't make your conclusion too short.
2. Don't use the same words as you used in the introduction when you summarize.
3. Don't write "The End."
4. Don't introduce new ideas that you didn't develop in the body of your essay.

Exercise 3. Writing and revising assignments: writing about a dream vacation   Imagine that you and your group members have won a contest. Your prize is a *twenty-four hour dream vacation!* You can go anywhere and do anything. Don't worry about money; all expenses will be paid! You can plan a trip to one place or you can plan a trip to several places. Your only limitation is that you have to do it all in twenty-four hours.

Step 1. Decide where you want to go for the morning, afternoon, and evening. Take notes of your discussion. Organize those notes into three categories: morning, afternoon, and evening.

Morning	Afternoon	Evening

Step 2. Talk about the details of the trip. Continue taking notes. How will you get to each place: car, plane, private jet, or limousine? What will you wear? Where will you eat? What will you do? Remember, the more details you have, the more interesting your writing will be. Choose what is most interesting to include.

Notes

Step 3. Now work by yourself. Write a first draft of your three body paragraphs. Think about what verb tense(s) you will use. Hint: it will be easier to write in the past tense as if you and your group members had already taken the trip. Be sure to write transition sentences so that you move smoothly from one part of the essay to the next part. Do not write the introduction or the conclusion yet.

_____

_____

_____

_____

_____

_____

_____

_____

Comments and Suggestions

 Step 4. Exchange what you have written with your group members. Read what others have written. Make notes on the bottom of their first draft. Tell them what you like best and what is not clear. Suggest whether any other information is needed.

Step 5. Read the comments on your own paper. Edit your paper.

Step 6. Write an introduction to your essay. Include one of the techniques listed in Exercise 2. Do the same for the conclusion of the essay.

Introduction:

_____

_____

_____

_____

_____

_____

_____

_____

_____

Conclusion:

_____

_____

_____

_____

_____

_____

_____

_____

_____

 Step 7. Exchange your essay draft with a partner. Is what you are reading clear? Is it interesting? Let your partner know. Talk about it.

Step 8. Rewrite your essay. Then submit it to your instructor.

Writing to Learn: *From Paragraph to Essay*

D Journal Assignment

Reading and writing reviews   Most newspapers feature reviews of movies, plays, concerts, recorded music, books, and restaurants. They are usually interesting reading, a good way to increase your vocabulary and a good source of ideas on how to spend your own free time.

Cut out a review from a newspaper or a magazine and read it carefully. Be sure it is a review and not an advertisement. Then fill out the following chart.

Source (name of newspaper or magazine, date)	
Subject (name of what was reviewed)	
Reviewer's opinion	
(Was it positive, negative, or mixed?)	
Positive words used in the review	
Negative words used in the review	
Your opinion about the review and the thing reviewed	

Now as a journal assignment, try writing your own review.

Other journal topics:

- The best vacation I have ever taken—describe it and/or write a postcard to someone
- The worst vacation I have ever taken—describe it and/or write a postcard to someone
- How I spend my free time—introduce your paragraph with a pie chart showing what percentage of your time is free time
- My collection of _____
- How people spend their free time in my country compared with how they do here
- Something I would like to do
- The best concert I ever attended
- An awful movie
- A good book

The Natural World

A Prewriting

1.

2.

My favorite place.

3.

4.

Exercise 1. Painting a picture in words   Write down as many names of things as you can for the first picture.

 Talk about the picture. Describe as precisely as you can what you see. Take turns giving your descriptions until you have talked about everything you can.

 Exercise 2. Comparing experience   Ask questions about the scene in the second picture. Write down any new words or expressions that you learn from your partner.

> EXAMPLE: Have you ever been hiking in the mountains?
>
> Where have you been on your hikes?
>
> Did you ever see a wild animal on your hikes?

New words or expressions

Exercise 3. Scientific language   Read this scientific explanation of why a rose is red. Focus on the language that is used to make the explanation scientific.

Why Is a Rose Red?

"Roses are red and violets are blue" are the words to a children's rhyme. Why is a rose red? Someone might think that a rose is red because that is its color. However, a rose is red because that is the color of the spectrum it reflects.

Color is the effect that is produced upon the eye and the nerves in the eye by light waves. The nerve cells in the retina of the eye that are sensitive to the different wavelengths of light are called rods and cones. Light stimulates different color cones, making perception of color possible.

Each light wave of color has a different wavelength. The spectrum of color is red, orange, yellow, green, blue, indigo, and violet. When light falls on an object, some of it is absorbed, and some of it is reflected. The color of an object depends on the wavelength that it reflects. A red object observed in daylight appears red because it reflects only the waves producing red light. A red rose is red because it reflects the red wavelength in daylight.

List the scientific words in the space provided.

Scientific words

Exercise 4. The red rose Look at the picture of the rose on page 136 (picture 3). Can you label the parts of the rose? Do you know the scientific name for a rose? Can you explain how a rose grows? How long does a rose live? Make notes in the space provided as you talk with the members of your group.

Parts of a rose	How a rose grows

Exercise 5. Thinking about nature For homework, go to the library and find a science book or a reference book. Look up your subject. Take notes on the next page. Be sure you do not just copy the exact words from the book.

Explain what you have learned about your subject to your classmates the next time your class meets.

Here are some things in nature that you might look into.

- a blue sky
- honey
- an elephant's trunk
- rising and falling tides

- autumn leaves
- thunder and lightning
- fog
- tidal waves

Subject: _____

Name of source: _____

Notes

_____

_____

_____

_____

_____

_____

_____

_____

_____

_____

_____

_____

_____

_____

_____

_____

_____

_____

_____

_____

_____

 Take turns in your group discussing what you learned from your research.

B Structure

Sentence Combining Chart

Relationship	Two independent clauses	Independent + dependent clause	Two independent clauses
Addition	**, and** I can sing well, **and** I can play the guitar well.		**also** I can sing well. I **also** can play the guitar well.
Cause and Effect	**, so** It rained, **so** the picnic was cancelled.	**because** The picnic was cancelled **because** it rained. **Because** it rained, the picnic was cancelled.	**; therefore,** It rained; **therefore,** the picnic was cancelled. It rained. **Therefore,** the picnic was cancelled.
Contrast	**, but** I tried, **but** I couldn't understand.	**although/even though/though** I couldn't understand **even though** I tried. **Even though** I tried, I couldn't understand.	**; however,** I tried; **however,** I couldn't understand. I tried. **However,** I couldn't understand.
Choice	**, or** You can fly to the East Coast, **or** you can drive there.		**on the other hand,** You can fly to the East Coast. **On the other hand,** you can drive there.
Time		**after/as soon as/ before, since/ when/whenever/ while** I have been thirsty **since** the movie started. **Since** the movie started, I have been thirsty.	**then/next** I got up. **Then** I took a shower.

Also, then, on the other hand

Use *also* to express a second idea that is similar to the first one you wrote.

EXAMPLE: I have been going to the beach for years. I have **also** been hiking in the mountains for a long time.

Use *then* to link two ideas by time order, the second coming after the first.

EXAMPLE: I went to the Grand Canyon. **Then,** I crossed the Mojave Desert.

Use *on the other hand* to contrast two ideas that are opposite or very different from each other.

EXAMPLE: Some people say fall is the prettiest season of the year. **On the other hand,** others say that spring is the prettiest.

Notice that these words show relationships between sentences, but often *do not* combine the sentences.

Note: There are many more ways to show relationships between sentences. These are only the ways practiced in this text.

Exercise 1. Using *also, then,* and *on the other hand* Rewrite these sentences using **also, then,** and **on the other hand.**

1. Carlos has been a member of the Sierra Club for two years. Carlos has been a member of Green Peace since 1990.

   _____

   _____

2. Pat studied botany in college. She worked in a plant nursery during her college years.

   _____

   _____

3. Dung flew across the Pacific Ocean when he was a high school student. He flew across the Atlantic Ocean the year he graduated from university.

   _____

   _____

4. Helene and Alex climbed Mt. McKinley by themselves. They tried to climb Mt. Everest without a guide.

_____

_____

5. Palm trees are native to California. The eucalyptus tree was brought to California from Australia.

_____

_____

6. Arturo and Ji Yun plan to surf in Hawaii if they can save enough money. If they are broke at the end of the semester, they will just go camping in the Sierras.

_____

_____

Exercise 2. Describing the geography of your country   Find your country on a map of the world. Show your classmates where it is. Tell them what countries are next to your own. Write six sentences with **also, then,** and **on the other hand** to describe the geography of your country. You might want to use some of the words listed here and other words that your teacher and classmates think of using.

mountains	plain	seaport
rivers	desert	volcano
lakes	jungle	delta
forest	valley	hills
wilderness	farmland	rural area

EXAMPLES: The northwestern United States has a wet climate and a lot of large forests. **On the other hand,** the southwestern United States has a dry climate with a lot of deserts.

If you like seaports, you should visit New York or Boston. **Then,** try Miami or New Orleans for warmer weather.

Hawaii is the only U.S. state with jungle. It is **also** one of the few states with an active volcano.

1. _____

   _____

2. _____

   _____

3. _____

   _____

4. _____

   _____

5. _____

   _____

6. _____

   _____

Exercise 3. More practice with *on the other hand* Write five sentences about controversial subjects or subjects that can be looked at from different perspectives. Then exchange books with your partner. Write a sentence with **on the other hand** to bring out the controversial aspect of the subject.

> **EXAMPLE:** You write: Nuclear energy is relatively clean and inexpensive.
>
> Your partner writes: **On the other hand,** it is very dangerous.

1. _____

   _____

2. _____

   _____

Writing to Learn: From Paragraph to Essay

3. _____

_____

4. _____

_____

5. _____

_____

Exercise 4. Editing for run-ons and fragments   Read the following sentences carefully. Write **RO** for run-on sentence. Write **F** for sentence fragment. Write **CS** for complete sentence. Correct the run-ons and fragments.

_____ 1. Many zoos are well run, on the other hand, some zoos are poorly designed for animals.

_____ 2. Dusk in the desert is a spectacular sight, also dawn.

_____ 3. I spent a week at the beach, then I went to the mountains.

_____ 4. Many people today depend on private automobiles for transportation, therefore air pollution is a problem in big cities.

_____ 5. When it snows.

_____ 6. There are many ways to learn about animals.

_____ 7. Then sun is necessary for life, but it can also be dangerous.

_____ 8. The U.S. National Park Service oversees several beautiful parks. For example, Yosemite.

Exercise 5. Exploring the natural world Discuss what you know about the following places and things. Then write a sentence for six of them, using one of the sentence combiners in the chart on page 141.

1. Mt. Everest
2. Mars
3. The sun
4. The Amazon River
5. Mount Fuji
6. The Grand Canyon

7. The North Pole
8. Tahiti
9. The Yucatan
10. Niagara Falls
11. (your idea) _____
12. (your idea) _____

1. _____

2. _____

3. _____

4. _____

5. _____

6. _____

C Writing and Editing

Exercise 1. Reading and analyzing an essay Read this essay carefully.

Morning on the Beach

I suppose that everyone has a favorite place. Mine is the beach. I don't mean the beach of umbrellas, suntan lotion, Frisbees, and radios. That is afternoon on the beach where every patch of sand is covered by blankets and chairs, and you can't hear the sea, only people talking. I mean morning on the beach. I try to get up as early as I can and walk the beach silently. There are no people in the early morning, only sandpipers, seals, pelicans, and hermit crabs. At that time of day, the

Writing to Learn: *From Paragraph to Essay*

quiet insistence of the waves that beat against the shore make me calm inside. I get a feeling of peace and strength from gazing out to the water, knowing that waves came to shore before I was here and will come to shore after I am gone.

I have often walked the beach on winter mornings just before sunrise. The morning sky looks like a palette of watercolors, though mostly blues, purples, grays, and yellows. When the sun comes over the horizon and brings the morning light, I can feel the meaning of the new day. It has really begun! The sun says so, and that is about as high an authority as I can think of. The sun gives more than morning light. It also brings warmth to the day and takes the sting out of the shore breeze. I share the sunrise with sandpipers and seagulls, who seem to be constantly looking for food at the water's edge. Every time I see a sandpiper I am reminded of a Japanese haiku poem in which "Sandpipers chase the sea and turning round are chased back again." I love that image because I know it so well.

Sometimes I get lucky on my morning walks and come across a seal who has decided to come ashore. Almost always, the seal has chosen a spot far away from the paths that lead down to the beach from the cliffs above. Almost always, the seal comes in at high tide when the water nearly covers the whole shoreline. I try to do two things when I spot a seal. One is to get closer so that I can see him better, and the second is to move slowly and silently so that I won't disturb him. Usually, the seal has found a perch on a small boulder and is intent on grooming himself in the early sunlight. Usually, he sees me no matter how quiet I think I am, and with a bark or two in my direction, he slides back into the water and out of sight. However, just the minute or two that I could look at him is enough to make me happy and somehow make that day special. I didn't see the seal in a zoo, clapping his flippers for fish. I saw him as he is in the natural world, a seal, not an entertainer.

There are times when I see seals and other creatures of the sea that make me very sad. It often happens like this. I am walking along the shoreline and I spot a large object. It doesn't look like a rock or a boat. I get a feeling inside that the object doesn't belong on the beach where it is because I know the contours of the shoreline so well. I come closer. I see gulls near the object. I start to smell something. It is the smell of decay. A hundred feet or so before I reach the object, I know it is a dead seal. I walk up to it to inspect the carcass. I see that around its neck is some sort of fishing net. Its body is swollen and its stomach has been ripped open by gulls. I know that seals, like humans, must die. What upsets me, though, is that the seal might have died as a result of getting trapped in a fishing net. It might have drowned in its own element, water. Fortunately for me, these times of sad discoveries are few. Most of the time I am happy when I walk the beach in the morning.

What is it that makes the beach such a special place for me? I was born and raised in New York City, in the concrete and asphalt of city life. Therefore, you couldn't say it was because of my childhood surroundings. On the other hand, my family used to spend summers in the country on an island with lots of beaches. I still remember those times and I cherish them. Another reason for my love of beaches might be that a few miles from my boyhood home was the city shoreline with its docks, ferries, and tankers. I could never swim in those waters or lie in what little sand there was, but I could look out into the waves and dream. Perhaps I was dreaming of the beaches I would one day walk on, on another coast.

Writing to Learn: *From Paragraph to Essay*

Answer the following questions about the essay.

1. Which of the following do you think is the topic of the essay?
    a. New York City, my hometown
    b. my favorite time and place
    c. the best beaches of the world
    d. the animals at the beach

2. Which sentence do you think carries the main idea of the essay?
    a. I suppose that everyone has a favorite place.
    b. My favorite place is morning on the beach.
    c. There are times when I see seals and other creatures of the sea that make me feel very sad.
    d. Perhaps I was dreaming of the beaches I would one day walk on another coast.

3. In the second paragraph, what idea about the beach does the author focus on?
    a. the beach is lonely
    b. birds on the beach
    c. Japanese poems
    d. morning on the beach in winter

4. In paragraph three, why does the author write about seals?
    a. They are in the zoo and at the beach.
    b. They are free and happy at the beach.
    c. They are entertainers.
    d. Seals are afraid of people.

5. In paragraph four, how does the author feel?
    a. happy
    b. trapped
    c. sad
    d. fortunate

6. Why does the author write about the dead seal?

   a. because you can be happy or sad in your favorite place

   b. because seals are dangerous

   c. because gulls are near the object

   d. because it doesn't look like a rock or boat

7. What is it that makes the beach a special place for the author?

   a. He used to spend summers at the beach, and he lived near a harbor.

   b. He grew up in an area of concrete and asphalt.

   c. He could never swim in the water near his house.

   d. He was born in New York City.

Exercise 2. Topic versus thesis By now you know that every paragraph needs to have a main idea or focus and a topic sentence. In an academic essay, the writer usually puts the main idea of the entire essay in the introductory paragraph. This main idea is called the thesis. It expresses the author's point of view or opinion about the topic. It is usually one sentence, although it can be more than one. The thesis may sometimes appear at the end of the introduction as well.

Every topic can have many different theses.

EXAMPLE: Topic: my favorite place

   Thesis 1:   My whole life has been tied to the sea, and it is the one place in this world where I feel completely myself.

   Thesis 2:   The bright lights, throbbing beat, and human crush of a big city nightclub make me feel alive.

   Thesis 3:   I glided off the ski lift through the pine trees to the Black Diamond Trail where I have spent so many thrilling hours.

   Thesis 4:   It's freezing cold and the wind almost knocks me off the top of the mountain, but there's no place else I'd rather be.

   Thesis 5:   Nestled between two rocky hills of heather is a quiet little meadow where I feel great peace.

   Thesis 6:   The sun is high in a clear blue sky dotted with one hundred-foot palm trees, and I am swimming laps at my favorite place, the city's outdoor pool.

Writing to Learn: *From Paragraph to Essay*

Write a thesis for each of these topics.

1. the most beautiful place in the world

_____

_____

2. pollution

_____

_____

3. cities

_____

_____

4. endangered animals

_____

_____

5. pesticides and food additives

_____

_____

Exercise 3. The thesis A thesis gives the writer's point of view about the topic. It can also express the organization of the essay.

> **EXAMPLE:** I have three favorite places. The first is Mount Sorak in Korea. The second is the city of Dubrovnik in Croatia. The third is Central Park in New York City.

Suppose the essay has five paragraphs: an introduction, three paragraphs in the body, and a conclusion. Then for each favorite place, there will be a separate paragraph.

Introduction: contains thesis

Paragraph 2: first place—Mount Sorak

Paragraph 3: second place—Dubrovnik

Paragraph 4: third place—Central Park

Conclusion: summary of main points with concluding idea

Write additional sentences for each thesis and make an outline of the essay as done earlier.

1. We have three kinds of pollution to worry about.

_____

_____

2. I have visited three of the world's most interesting cities.

_____

_____

3. There are three reasons to protect our natural environment.

_____

_____

Outline:

_____

_____

_____

_____

_____

Exercise 4. Editing with *also, then,* and *on the other hand*   Reread the essay. Decide whether you could use **also, then,** or **on the other hand** to express a second similar idea, a fact or event that follows after the first, or a contrasting idea or example. You might just add one of the words or you might remove a phrase or word and use **also, then,** and **on the other hand** instead.

EXAMPLE: I didn't see the seal in a zoo, clapping his flippers for fish. I saw him as he is in the natural world, a seal, not an entertainer.

Edited version: I didn't see the seal in a zoo, clapping his flippers for fish. **On the other hand, I did see** him as he is in the natural world, a seal, not an entertainer.

Compare the two sentences. What difference does separating the sentences with *on the other hand* make? Notice that the verb was changed from *saw* to *did see*. This adds emphasis to the contrast between the seal in the zoo and the seal in nature. This sort of difference is one of style, not grammar. As you develop your writing, you develop a unique voice, your own style.

EXAMPLE: Its body is swollen and its stomach has been ripped open by gulls.

Edited version: *Its body is swollen. Its stomach has **also** been ripped open by gulls.*

Exercise 5. Writing assignment: my favorite place   You are going to write an essay about your favorite place. Follow the steps below.

Step 1. Return to the pictures on page 136. In the blank space (picture 4), draw as well as you can your favorite place in nature. Put as much detail as you can into the drawing. Do not worry if it is not a perfect reproduction of that place. Just do your best.

Step 2. Describe your favorite place, too, using your drawing to help you describe and explain. Then, listen to your partner's description. As you look at your partner's drawing and listen to him or her speak, do any other words occur to you? If they do, tell them to your partner. Use the following questions to help you talk about your picture.

1. Where is your favorite place?

2. What do you do there?

3. Who do you go with?

4. How often do you go there?

5. When was the last time you were there?

6. What did you do?

7. What is your favorite thing about the place?

Step 3. Write a paragraph describing your drawing.

_____

_____

_____

_____

_____

_____

Unit 6: The Natural World

_____

_____

_____

_____

_____

_____

_____

_____

_____

_____

_____

Step 4. Write a thesis statement for an essay about your favorite place.

_____

_____

Step 5. Brainstorm ways to expand your writing from paragraph to essay. What ideas do you want to express? How many paragraphs will they form? You need five paragraphs for this essay.*

Paragraph 1: introduction, which contains your thesis

Paragraph 2: developing the first idea

Paragraph 3: developing the second idea

Paragraph 4: developing the third idea

Paragraph 5: conclusion, which summarizes ideas and shows how you proved your thesis

*Remember each paragraph in the body needs a topic sentence.

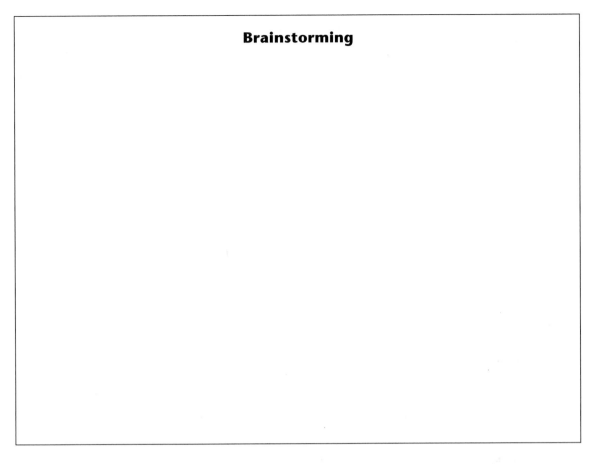

Brainstorming

Step 6. On a piece of paper, write a first draft of your essay.

Exercise 6. Revising your essay   Make three copies of your draft so that each person in your group has a copy. Then, follow these steps.

Step 1.
a. Read each essay at home.
b. Use a pencil to edit each essay.
c. Put a line through any sentence that you think could be cut from the essay.
d. Join two sentences in each paragraph with one of the combining words you have learned in this text (see chart on page 141).

Step 2. In class, work with one group member at a time. Share your ideas about revising the draft. Spend at least ten minutes with each paper. At the end of class, give back to each person your copy of his or her draft with corrections, changes, and editing on it.

Step 3. At home, use your classmates' suggestions to revise your own essay. Bring it in to the next class. Read the revised essay to your group. Take ten minutes each to discuss the revisions. Take notes from the discussion.

Step 4. Write a final draft to turn in to your instructor.

D Journal Assignment

Choose from these journal topics. If you have email, send one of your journal entries to a friend. If everyone in your class has email, write email messages to each other instead of writing them in your journal.

- What I do to preserve the environment
- What animal I am most like
- My fantasy garden
- The earth in 100 years
- How technology harms nature
- How technology benefits nature
- Nature in the city

Appendix I

Nouns, Verbs, Pronouns, Adjectives, and Adverbs

- A **noun** is a person, place, or thing. Things can be abstract, nonmaterial. For example, *truth* and *beauty* are nouns.

    EX: that **student, Mr. Smith, you** *(person)*

    New York City, my **room,** the **gym** *(place)*

    a good **book,** our **dog,** his final exam **grade** *(thing)*

- A noun can be a subject or an object. The subject does the action and the object receives the action.

    EX: My **sister** studies **French** in **Canada.**
                subject   object   object of preposition

- A **verb** is an action or a state of being.

    EX: eat, sleep, think *(action)*

    seem, feel, be *(state of being)*

- Some verbs combine with other verbs to create meaning with verb tense. They are **auxiliary verbs.**

    EX: He **is** going to the concert.

    Moira **has** seen that movie.

- A **pronoun** takes the place of a noun.

    EX: My **teacher** is a nice person. **She** is a nice person.
               noun   pronoun

Subject Pronouns		Object Pronouns	
I	we	me	us
you	you	you	you
he/she/it	they	him/her/it	them

Possessive Adjectives		Possessive Pronouns	
my	our	mine	ours
your	your	yours	yours
his/her/its	their	his/hers	theirs

Reflexive Pronouns	
myself	ourselves
yourself	yourselves
himself/herself/itself	themselves

- An **adjective** is a word that describes the quality of something. Adjectives usually come before the noun.

  EX: It was a **beautiful** day.
          adjective

- An **adverb** is a word that describes a verb. Adverbs usually come after a verb and often end in *-ly*.

  EX: I did my work **carefully.**
          adverb

  He worked **hard.**
          adverb

Appendix II

The Traditional Twelve Verb Tenses

English has twelve tenses according to many traditional grammar books. They are in chart form below.

Aspect → Time ↓	Simple	Perfect	Progressive (or continuous)	Perfect Progressive
past	John **saw** a good movie.	John **had seen** the movie (before he read the book).	John **was watching** TV (when the doorbell rang).	John **had been watching** TV (when the fire started).
present	John **reads** poetry.	John **has seen** that movie.	John **is watching** TV.	John **has been watching** TV all day long.
future	John **will read** (is going to) the report tomorrow.	John **will have seen** that movie (before it leaves town).	John **will be watching** TV (when I get home).	John **will have been watching** TV for ten hours by midnight.

Common irregular verb forms

Base Form	Irregular Past Form	Irregular Past Participles
be	was, were	been
become	became	become
begin	began	begun
break	broke	broken
bring	brought	brought
build	built	built

(Continued)

Base Form	Irregular Past Form	Irregular Past Participles
buy	bought	bought
catch	caught	caught
choose	chose	chosen
come	came	come
cost	cost	cost
cut	cut	cut
do	did	done
draw	drew	drawn
eat	ate	eaten
fall	fell	fallen
feed	fed	fed
feel	felt	felt
fight	fought	fought
find	found	found
fly	flew	flown
forget	forgot	forgotten
forgive	forgave	forgiven
get	got	gotten
give	gave	given
go	went	gone
grow	grew	grown
have	had	had
hear	heard	heard
hide	hid	hidden
hit	hit	hit

Base Form	Irregular Past Form	Irregular Past Participles
hold	held	held
hurt	hurt	hurt
keep	kept	kept
know	knew	known
lay	laid	laid
lead	led	led
leave	left	left
lend	lent	lent
let	let	let
lose	lost	lost
make	made	made
mean	meant	meant
meet	met	met
pay	paid	paid
put	put	put
quit	quit	quit
read	read	read
ride	rode	ridden
ring	rang	rung
rise	rose	risen
run	ran	run
say	said	said
see	saw	seen
sell	sold	sold
send	sent	sent

(Continued)

Appendix

Base Form	Irregular Past Form	Irregular Past Participles
set	set	set
shake	shook	shaken
show	showed	shown/showed
sing	sang	sung
sit	sat	sat
sleep	slept	slept
speak	spoke	spoken
spend	spent	spent
stand	stood	stood
steal	stole	stolen
swim	swam	swum
swing	swung	swung
take	took	taken
teach	taught	taught
tell	told	told
think	thought	thought
throw	threw	thrown
understand	understood	understood
wake	woke	woken
wear	wore	worn
win	won	won
write	wrote	written

Appendix III

Verb + Gerund and Verb + Infinitive

Here is a more complete list of verbs that take a gerund or an infinitive or both gerund and infinitive.

Verbs that take gerund -ing	Verbs that take infinitive to	Verbs that take both gerund and infinitive
admit	afford	begin
appreciate	agree	(can/can't) bear
consider	appear	continue
delay	arrange	forget*
deny	ask	hate
discuss	attempt	like
dislike	beg	love
enjoy	care	plan
excuse	choose	prefer
face	come	pretend
feel like	dare	propose
finish	decide	regret
mention	expect	remember*
(do/don't) mind	hope	start
miss	learn	stop*
postpone	manage	try*
practice	mean	
put off	need	
resist	neglect	
risk	offer	
(can/can't) stand	prepare	
suggest	promise	
understand	refuse	
	seem	
	want	
	wish	

*These verbs have a different meaning when used with the infinitive or the gerund.

Appendix IV
Sentence Combining Chart

Relationship	Two independent clauses	Independent + dependent clause	Two independent clauses
Addition	**, and** I can sing well, **and** I can play the guitar well.		**also** I can sing well. I **also** can play the guitar well.
Cause and effect	**, so** It rained, **so** the picnic was cancelled.	**because** The picnic was cancelled **because** it rained. **Because** it rained, the picnic was cancelled.	**; therefore,** It rained; **therefore,** the picnic was cancelled. It rained. **Therefore,** the picnic was cancelled.
Contrast	**, but** I tried, **but** I couldn't understand.	**although/even though/though** I couldn't understand **even though** I tried. **Even though** I tried, I couldn't understand.	**; however,** I tried; **however,** I couldn't understand. I tried. **However,** I couldn't understand.
Choice	**, or** You can fly to the East Coast, **or** you can drive there.		**on the other hand,** You can fly to the East Coast. **On the other hand,** you can drive there.
Time		**after/as soon as/before, since/when/whenever/while** I have been thirsty **since** the movie started. **Since** the movie started, I have been thirsty.	**then/next** I got up. **Then** I took a shower.

Writing to Learn: *From Paragraph to Essay*

Appendix V

Form of Titles

- Capitalize the first word.
- Capitalize all words except articles (e.g., **a, an, the**) and prepositions (e.g., **to, from, at**). Pronouns are usually capitalized.
- Remember that countries, languages, and people from countries are always capitalized (e.g., American, French, Korean).
- Do not use a period (.) at the end, but you may need a question mark (?) or an exclamation mark (!).
- Center a title.

Appendix VI

Basic Rules of Capitalization

Capitalize:

- The first word in a sentence

    EX: **G**orillas are animals that live in Africa.

- The pronoun *I*, but no other pronoun unless it begins a sentence

    EX: **I** discovered that **I** like to write.

- The first letter of the first word in quoted speech

    EX: She asked, "**W**ho is coming to dinner tonight?"

- The first letter of a noun when it goes with the specific name of a person, place, or thing

    EX: **S**ecretary **S**mith of the **U**nited **N**ations visited the **E**iffel **T**ower yesterday.

- Every word except conjunctions, articles, and short prepositions in the titles of books, movies, plays, magazines, and other written works

    EX: **F**innegan, the **H**ero

- If the conjunction, article, or preposition is the first word of a title, then you must capitalize it.

    EX: **A** Gloomy Afternoon
          In Springtime

- The names of languages, nationalities, countries, cities, towns, and villages

    EX: The **S**panish of **M**exicans from **E**l **S**itio in **Z**acatecas, **M**exico is different from the **S**panish of **S**paniards from **M**adrid, **S**pain.

Appendix VII
Basic Rules of Punctuation

Punctuation

- A period goes at the end of a sentence or after the last letter of an abbreviation. Remember not to use a period after a title.

  EX: I received a letter from Mr. John Jones. It was dated one month ago.

- Use a comma before conjunctions when they join two independent clauses.

  EX: I tried calling Burt at his office, but nobody answered the phone.

- Use a comma when a dependent clause comes first.

  EX: After Marie filled out the application, she mailed it.

- Use a comma to set off dates, addresses, and titles.

  EX: Dr. John Lincoln, Professor of Modern Music, died at his home in Cleveland, Ohio, on March 23, 1999.

- Use a comma to separate words, phrases, and clauses in a series.

  EX: Dina likes mango, papaya, passion fruit, and guava.

  Bob complained about the bad weather, his dreary office job, and his boring life.

- Use a comma to separate adjectives that follow one another.

  EX: It was an old, dark, frightening room.

- Use a semicolon to separate two independent clauses when they are not joined by a coordinating conjunction or when they are joined by a conjunctive adverb.

  EX: Nuvia loved to work with her hands; she was a marvelous seamstress.

  Il Bum had always wanted to travel to Niagara Falls; however, he had never had the time to make the trip.

- Use a colon after the greeting in a business letter or a formal letter.

  EX: Dear Dr. Gonzalez:

- Use quotation marks to set off direct speech.

  EX: Ernesto said, "Makiko, you look beautiful today."

- Use an apostrophe to indicate possession.

  EX: That is Lou's guitar.

- Use an apostrophe to show that a letter or letters is missing from a word.

  EX: He couldn't have been here in '99.

Appendix VIII
Basic Form of a Paragraph

The basic form of a paragraph follows these rules:

- Indent at the beginning of a paragraph.

- Leave a margin on the left and on the right.

- Use 1.5 or 2 line spaces when word processing, or skip a line when writing longhand.

- Use one space after a comma and two spaces after a period when word processing. When writing longhand, be sure to leave space after a period to separate sentences.

- One sentence follows another with no space in between.

EX: When I was a little boy, my mother used to walk me to school. She told me never to cross the busy city streets by myself. My school was only two blocks away from my home, but my mother used to say, "Don't cross those streets by yourself. It's too dangerous." So I listened to her. One day my mother was sick. She asked a friend's mother to stop by our house and take me to school. The woman forgot about me. My mother was sick in bed, but she started to dress. I said, "Mom, you're too sick to take me. I'm big enough to cross by myself." That was the first time I crossed a city street by myself. I was five years old.

Appendix IX
Suggestions for Success in College Writing Classes

All of your work should look professional.

1. Buy standard size paper (8 1/2 by 11 with lines) with three holes and keep it in a binder.

2. Every paper must have a heading. Some teachers have a required style. If your teacher does not tell you how to head your paper, you can use the form shown on page 168.

Sample Paper

Betty Mannion
Writing 119, M. Spaventa
Essay #6
May 15, 2000

My Favorite Place

In this hectic world everybody needs to relax, and most people look forward to enjoying their favorite place in their free time. I do, too. My favorite place is my home.

My home is the only place where I can feel like a queen in my own kingdom because in my home I make myself comfortable, powerful, and safe. I always do anything I want. At home I make all kinds of decisions about cleaning, shopping, cooking, and making plans for vacations. I love it.

Usually, every morning as soon as I clean my house carefully, I like to read the newspaper in my back yard. After everybody is gone, it is fantastic to have a little free time to enjoy the sun, drink some tea, and read the news in my quiet, lovely home.

In my favorite place, the kitchen is my favorite room. I like to bake cookies, pies, and cakes. Also I am always excited about experimenting with some new recipes. I really enjoy cooking because I try to give my family a gift of good meals. While I cook, I can see my beautiful garden and roses through my window. I love my kitchen. It is small, but big enough for me. I can't wait until my son and my husband come home. Then we can have dinner together and talk about our day or discuss the current news. Right away after we finish dinner, I clean my kitchen while watching my husband and my son playing in the backyard.

Maybe for some people it sounds boring, but for me, my home is my favorite place. I love to see my kitchen and the rest of the house looking very clean. It makes me feel great when I spend a long time at home doing my best for my family and for the place where I live. It is the place where I enjoy the best I have: my family.

3. Do not write in the margins on the left and right side of the paper. (Most notebook paper has a red or blue line to show the margin.)

4. Some teachers want you to skip lines or write on every other line.

5. Your teacher will tell you if you should use pencil or pen. If you use pencil, make sure your teacher can see it! Use a computer whenever possible.

Cheating and Plagiarism

Cheating and plagiarism are very serious matters in North American classrooms! Please do not cheat or plagiarize.

Cheating is looking at another student's paper for the answers on a quiz or test, or looking in your book or at papers for answers when you take a test. Copying another student's homework is also cheating.

Plagiarism is copying the words from a book and presenting them as your own words. You need to use quotation marks "..." when you use the words from a book or someone else's words. The North American definition of plagiarism is often difficult for students to understand. Also, you cannot copy another student's essay or paper and put your name on it.

Appendix X
Journal Writing

Journals are notebooks in which writers keep a record of ideas, opinions, and descriptions of daily life. Journals help writers develop their creativity. In writing classes, instructors often ask students to write in journals.

Each writing instructor has different ideas about journal writing. Your instructor will tell you how to keep your journal and will probably collect it at certain times during the semester. Your instructor may write reactions to what you write and offer suggestions for vocabulary or improving your grammar. However, the main point of keeping a journal as a language student is to give you a chance to write about your ideas without worrying about a grade or correct grammar. Journal writing is practice in writing and thinking.

Buy a standard size notebook with lined paper. Make this notebook your journal for this writing class only. Write nothing else in it. Do not write other class assignments in your journal. There are many rewards from keeping a journal, in addition to the informal conversation that takes place in it between you and yourself, and you and your instructor: when you have finished the course, you will have a record of what you read, what you experienced, and what you thought about during that time.

At the end of each chapter in this book, you will find some topics related to the theme of the unit. Write about them in your journal.

Appendix XI
Academic Vocabulary

It is important to know these terms when planning your academic future. Match the following vocabulary words with the best definition.

- **enroll**   to register for a class or course of study

- **transfer**   to change from one school to another

- **major**   a specialization in college

- **career**   a field of employment; a profession

- **high school diploma**   a document that indicates completion of high school

- **GED**   in the United States, a certificate of high school equivalency that indicates a student has passed an examination

- **certificate**   an official document showing that a student has completed a course of studies

- **A.A. or A.S. degree**   Associate of Arts/Associate of Science; a document of completion from a two-year college

- **B.A. or B.S. degree**   Bachelor of Arts/Bachelor of Science; a document of completion from a four-year college

- **M.A. or M.S. degree**   Master of Arts/Master of Science; a document of completion of academic studies beyond the B.A. or B.S. level

- **Ph.D. degree**   Doctor of Philosophy; a document of completion of the highest level of study in a university

- **credit**   a unit of course work

- **required course**   a course that must be taken

- **prerequisite**   a course that must be taken before taking another course

- **due date**   the last day to hand in an assignment; a deadline

- **financial aid**   money from a school or college to help a student pay for tuition or books: work-study, a loan, or a scholarship

- **scholarship**   an award of money from a school or college to help a student pay for tuition or books; the student does not need to repay a scholarship

- **G.P.A.**   grade point average—the average of a student's grades

Writing to Learn: *From Paragraph to Essay*

G.P.A. can be calculated for one semester or for all the courses taken. This is sometimes called your cumulative G.P.A. Most schools in the United States calculate G.P.A. in this way.

A = 4 points   B = 3 points   C = 2 points   D = 1 point   F = 0 points

EX: Reading   B   (3 points) $\times$ 3 units*   =   9 points

Writing   A   (4 points) $\times$ 3 units   = 12 points

Spanish   D   (1 point) $\times$ 3 units   =   3 points

Math   C   (3 points) $\times$ 3 units   =   9 points

                                 12 units   33 points

Now divide points by units. G.P.A. = 2.75

*Each course carries 3 units in this example. However, some courses may be 1, 2, 4, or even 6 units.

Appendix XII

Sample Application for Employment in the United States

Please note that applications vary from state to state and company to company.

Position Desired _____

Personal

(Please use blue or black ink and print clearly.)

Name _____
            first name   middle initial   last name

*Social Security Number _____

Street Address _____ Apt. No. or Box _____

City _____ State _____ Zip Code _____

Telephone Number _____

Are you 18 or older?   ☐ Yes   ☐ No

*Please note a social security number is required to work in the United States.

(Continued)

Education

School most recently attended:

Name _____ Location _____

Graduated? ☐ Yes   ☐ No

If no, last grade completed _____

Now enrolled? ☐ Yes   ☐ No

Sports or Activities _____

_____

_____

_____

_____

Work Experience

Three most recent jobs within the last five years

Company _____ Position _____

Dates worked: From _____ To _____

Salary _____ Supervisor _____

Reason for leaving _____

_____

Company _____ Position _____

Dates worked: From _____ To _____

Salary _____ Supervisor _____

Reason for leaving _____

_____

(Continued)

Writing to Learn: *From Paragraph to Essay*

Company _____ Position _____

Dates worked: From _____ To _____

Salary _____ Supervisor _____

Reason for leaving _____

_____

General

Date available _____ Total hours available per week _____

Check any that apply: ☐ Full-time   ☐ Part-time   ☐ Day shift   ☐ Night shift

Do you have any physical condition or handicap that
may limit your ability to perform the job applied for?   ☐ Yes   ☐ No

If yes, what can be done to accommodate your limitation? _____

_____

Have you ever been convicted of a felony?   ☐ Yes   ☐ No

Are you a veteran?   ☐ Yes   ☐ No

List the names of three references whom we can contact who have knowledge of your
skills, talents, or technical knowledge.

1. _____
   Name and Relationship (Supervisor, Teacher, etc.)   Phone Number

2. _____
   Name / Relationship   Phone Number

3. _____
   Name / Relationship   Phone Number

*I certify, by my signature below, that any false or omitted important facts in my answers
on this application may be cause for dismissal.*

_____
Applicant's Signature   Date

Glossary

base form   The base form is also called the simple form. It is the infinitive without *to*. It is the form you would find in a dictionary.

   EXAMPLE: *go*

brainstorming   This means getting all of your ideas on paper or on the board without organizing or evaluating them.

coordinating conjunctions   (*and, but, so, or*) These are words that join independent clauses. Conjunctions typically join sentences that are equal in importance. Use a comma before a coordinating conjunction.

   EXAMPLE: *I have read the book, but I haven't seen the movie.*

dependent clause   This is a group of words that includes a subject and verb, but does not make a complete sentence by itself. A dependent clause begins with a subordinator. It must be combined with an independent clause in written English.

   EXAMPLE: ***When I was a child,*** *I loved to read.*

edit   To edit is to find and correct mistakes to improve your writing.

essay   An essay is a short piece of writing, very often consisting of at least five paragraphs. Essays typically include an introduction of one paragraph, a body of three or more paragraphs, and a conclusion of one paragraph. In academic essays, importance is placed on expressing a point of view using examples and logic. Students in North American colleges and universities are frequently required to write essays.

focus   The focus is the main idea of a paragraph.

fragment   A fragment is an incomplete sentence, often a dependent clause.

   EXAMPLE: *When I read his essay.*

freewriting   This is writing that is designed to improve fluency and spontaneity. The main idea is to write as much as possible without correcting or editing. Freewriting is also called quickwriting.

independent clause   This clause is made up of a group of words that include a subject and verb. An independent clause is a complete sentence by itself. It can be connected to a dependent clause, or it can be connected to another independent clause.

   EXAMPLES: *I love to read. When I was a child,* ***I loved to read. I love to read,*** *and* ***I enjoy writing.***

peer editing   Peer editing is helping a classmate or friend to improve her or his writing. A peer is your equal, in this case, a classmate.

preposition   These are small words that show location, direction and time, and combine with nouns as their objects.

   EXAMPLES: *to the store, in the classroom, at the movies, on the desk, from Vancouver, over there.*

prepositional phrase   A prepositional phrase is a group of words beginning with a preposition followed by a noun phrase.

   EXAMPLES: ***in*** *high school,* ***to*** *the store*

question word order Normal question word order is (Question word) + verb + subject *or* (Question word) + auxiliary verb + subject + verb.

> **EXAMPLES:** *Where was he? Where did he go?*

question words *who(m), what, when, where, which, why, how, how long* are question words. They are also called information question words because they ask for specific information, not a yes or no answer.

> **EXAMPLE:** *Who is sitting next to Jean?* Answer: *Marie.*

revise To revise is to add or cut ideas from your writing to make it more clear and focused. Revising is usually done before editing for grammar, spelling, and punctuation mistakes.

run-on sentence Two sentences that are written together without proper punctuation, coordination, or subordination are combined. This is called a run-on sentence.

> **EXAMPLE:** *Ms. Goodnough was my favorite teacher she always made us laugh.*

statement word order Normal subject word order is subject + verb (+ object) (verb phrase).

> **EXAMPLE:** *I love English.*

subordinating conjunction These conjunctions are also called conjunctive adverbs. They include *after, before, when, as soon as, since, while, whenever, because, although, even though,* and *though.* Subordinating conjunctions introduce dependent clauses.

> **EXAMPLE:** ***When I was a child,*** *I loved to read.* ***Because I read so much,*** *writing is easy for me.*

thesis The thesis is the main idea or point of view of an essay expressed in one or more sentences, usually in the introductory paragraph of an essay or in the first few lines of a paragraph.

title The introductory phrase to a paragraph, essay, story, or book is the title. It is usually not a complete sentence. The title should capture the reader's attention or imagination.

topic The main idea or subject about which one writes is called the topic.

topic sentence The topic sentence shows the main idea or the point of view of a paragraph. It limits the focus of the paragraph.

transition A transition is another word for an adverbial conjunction. Some transitions are *however, therefore, nevertheless, moreover, thus, as a result, otherwise,* and *consequently.* Transitions can be used to relate two independent clauses with a period.

> **EXAMPLES:** *I have worked through this entire text;* ***therefore,*** *my writing has improved.*
>
> *My writing has improved a lot.* ***However,*** *I know that I have even more to learn.*